John Ireland

Letters and poems by the late Mr. John Henderson

With anecdotes of his life

John Ireland

Letters and poems by the late Mr. John Henderson
With anecdotes of his life

ISBN/EAN: 9783742827067

Manufactured in Europe, USA, Canada, Australia, Japa

Cover: Foto ©Andreas Hilbeck / pixelio.de

Manufactured and distributed by brebook publishing software
(www.brebook.com)

John Ireland

Letters and poems by the late Mr. John Henderson

L O N D O N:

PRINTED FOR J. JOHNSON, NO. 72, ST. PAUL'S
CHURCH-YARD.

M.DCC.LXXXVI.

PREFACE.

OUR Second Charles, of pleafant and good-natured memory, obferving Gregorio Leti, the Italian hiftorian, attending his levee, afked him how his book went on; for, faid the King, " I am informed you intend publifhing Anecdotes of the En-glifh Court. Take care there be no offence in it." " Sire," anfwered the Italian, " I am collecting materials for fuch a work,

 and

and will be careful as poſſible ; but, unleſs a man be wiſe as Solomon, he cannot publiſh Anecdotes without giving ſome offence." "Why then," replied the Monarch " cannot you be wiſe as Solomon ? write *Proverbs* and let *Anecdotes* alone."

The counſel was good, and counſel have I alſo received.

I was told, he that wrote of thoſe who were living, or *ſtept upon aſhes which were not yet cold,* ought not to inſert his name in the title page ; for it was committing him-ſelf, and might create enemies. The advice had influence, but not the influence which was intended. Conſcious of meaning to

publiſh

publish truth, and truth only, I venture to prefix my name to this book.

The person of whom I write, had once my warmest partiality, and living with him in habits of the most unreserved intimacy, I knew him well. The motives which actuated his conduct, are explained in his letters; that I now possess them, and the fragments of poetry which he gave me, is owing, in some measure to accident, and, in some degree, to a habit I have of preserving any thing, however trifling, which is the production of a friend. On my once shewing a number of little sketches by the late Mr. Mortimer, a gentleman asked me, if I had hoarded up the cuttings of his pencils.

From

From Mr. Henderſon's letters, I have endeavoured to ſelect ſuch as tend to explain
his theatrical ſtory, or ſuch as from their
naïveté, pleaſantry, and good ſenſe, place
his powers in a light, which, I think, gives
them a diſtinguiſhed rank in that claſs of
writing.   It is ſcarce neceſſary to premiſe,
that they were not intended for the preſs,
and therefore exhibit, *not* the writer and his
labours, but the *man* in his natural character.

I am apprehenſive it may be thought that
ſome of them are unimportant, and relate to
private tranſactions, with which the public
have no concern, and that I might have
compreſſed the volume, by omitting the in-
troductions and concluſions of thoſe to myſelf,

felf, which frequently contain merely a repetition of the fame profeffions of friendfhip, only expreffed in different words; but I think, that originality of turn which he frequently gives to the moft trifling circumftance, fuch a mark of his mind, as ought not to be withheld by him who profeffes to publifh his letters; and I am inclined to look upon that editor who lops off, at his own difcretion, any branches with which he happens to be diffatisfied, as fometimes doing more than his duty warrants.

There are fome mifcellaneous epiftles written at a very early period of his life: the few which I have inferted that were addreffed to him, need not any apology for their publication.

The poems which are subjoined, considered as hasty effusions rather than finished
compositions, as the productions of a
man who had received few aids from
education,* and whose only guides were a
classical taste, formed by having read, with

a power

* It is not intended to insinuate this as an apology.
I thought they had merit, or I would not have published
them.   Nothing can be more contemptible than pester-
ing the public with reams of nonsense, by young gentlemen under fourteen years of age, black women, men-
mercers, ostlers who cannot spell; and esquires, who
can do little more.

If a work has merit enough for the public eye, that
public will generally protect and encourage it; and if it
has not, its being written while the author was standing
upon one leg, or standing upon his head; written with

his

a power of difcrimination, fome of the beft
Englifh writers, prove that he poffeffed imagination, and aptitude of poetical expreffion,
which might, had he made poefy the object
of his purfuit, have been cultivated into
excellence.

Attached to his previous reputation, they
may excite curiofity, and, I hope, gratify it,
by exhibiting his talents in a new point of
view.

The high eftimation in which his abilities
were held by men of diftinguifhed rank
in literature, the ample teftimony which

was

his fingers, or written with his toes ; written in feven
days, or feven months, are very infufficient reafons to
give for its appearance, in an age when the prefs teems
with hourly births, of which we only know, that " *they
were born, and died.*"

was given to his merit as an actor, and the eminent honours which were paid to his memory as a man, firſt ſuggeſted the idea of publiſhing his letters and poems. I reviewed what had my early approbation, and time has not much funk them in my opinion.

It has been ſuggeſted to me, that my notes are too numerous, and too long, but I could not well abridge, or incorporate them with the work. 'Tis the error of inexperience; for this is the firſt book I ever ventured before the awful tribunal of the public. If I have pardon from my readers, and ſhould ever publiſh another, that fault ſhall be avoided.

ANECDOTES

Mr. JOHN HENDERSON.

A CLAIM of literary honours, for men who have not received a fcho-laftic education, is, I am confcious, liable to be contefted.* The avenues to that portal of the Temple of fame, are guarded by the giants of learning, who, mounted upon pedeftals, compofed of huge tomes

of

---

* It feems a general axiom, that he who has never felt *birch*, fhould never wear *bays*.

of folios, quartos, and duodecimos, which only prove, *that men were dull in ancient days*, look down with sullen contempt on the adventurer who is hardy enough to attempt gaining accefs, through any other than the prefcribed and beaten path.

This temple, as was that of the Druids, is kept facred from the intrufion of the un-hallowed multitude, and the unanealed man, who attempts to fnatch a fprig of the holy mifletoe, is in fome danger of being facrificed upon the altar, as a propitiatory offer-ing to the offended deity of the place.

Of thofe whofe eminence hath been thought worthy of Biography, we frequently read, that they received the rudiments of their education from one learned man, and were affifted by the inftructions of another,

then

then configned to an univerfity, where they added to their claffic knowledge, and *rich in the ftores of ancient Greece and Rome* burft into fociety, where they were gazed at with the eye of expectation, and gratified with reiterated praife.

Indeed thefe gentlemen do not *always* give indications of having obtained many advantages by their ftudies, yet are they fpoken of, as men who from their education muft be in poffeffion of great powers, if they could but be prevailed upon to exert them.

Very different was the introduction of Mr. Henderfon; of Greek he was totally ignorant, and little acquainted with Latin.*

He

---

* A fhort time before he went to Bath, a clergyman, by whofe partiality I am honoured, and who has kindly

 permitted

He had no claim to hereditary honours, nor title to any paternal inheritance. + He was the builder of his own fame, and the founder of his own fortune, for had not his talents brought him into celebrity, and given him the power of acquiring independence, it is not probable that any one would have enquired who was his grandfather.

permitted me to enhance the value of this volume by the publication of one of his letters, pointed out the course of his ftudies, and gave him fome affiftance in an attempt to attain that language; but Henderfon's mind was too volatile for the *gradus ad Parnaffum.*

+ It has been faid he was defcended from Doctor Alexander Henderfon, of Fordyll; for this there is no authority, except the name being fpelt in the fame manner. He believed his family were originally Irifh, but whether they were or not, he neither knew nor cared. He thought, with Sir Thomas Overbury, that the man who has nothing to boaft of but his illuftrious anceftry, is fomewhat like a potatoe, the only good thing is under ground.

father. Of his grandfather, however, thofe who wifh it may read in the Memoirs of an unfortunate young Nobleman, by which Memoirs, and fome collateral evidence, it appears that he was a Quaker, and a warm adherent to the caufe of Mr. Annefley. That in conjunction with feveral others, he adventured a confiderable fum in fupport of the Anglefey lawfuit, which being loft, the money advanced was never recovered by himfelf or Henderfon's father, who was an Irifh factor in Goldfmith-ftreet, Cheapfide, where Mr. John Henderfon was born in February 1746-7.

By his father's death in 1748, his mother was left with a very flender pittance, and two fons totally dependent upon her. She retired to Newport Pagnell, where a clofe attention to œconomy enabled her to

B 3

fupport

support herself and family upon the interest of less than a thousand pounds. *

In this place, with no other tutor than his mother, Henderson passed the early part of his life. She taught him to read, pointed out the proper authors, and induced him to imprint upon his memory, and recite, select passages from Shakespeare, Pope, Addison, or any other English classic in her possession.

The

* The eldest son she apprenticed to a Mr. Clee, an ingenious engraver, in Oxendon-street, and the young man gave early promise of great professional talents; but being of a very delicate habit, fell into a decline, and was removed to Paddington, where happening to lodge in the same house with the afterwards celebrated Kitty Fisher, and being suddenly seized with a violent fit of coughing, the good-natured girl ran to his assistance, and he died in her arms.

The wonder-working magic of the old bard inchanted his imagination, * opened a new creation to his fancy, and prompted him to enquire how thofe characters were reprefented which afforded him fo much delight in the perufal. The defcription promoted a moft eager wifh to fee a play, a wifh which could not then be gratified, for in Newport-Pagnell there were no players.

Learning and reciting the fpeeches improved a memory naturally tenacious, and gave him an early relifh for polite literature.

B 4

By

---

* The firft play which attracted and delighted him, was, *The Winter's Tale*, and he often declared it was fortunate for him, the commentators had not been about his mother's edition. It was without notes; which, faid he, confufe, perplex, and embarrafs me *now*. God help me, what would they have done *then?* I fuppofe they would have crazed *me*, as they have other people.

By this was his taste formed, and as the writer of these ˎ anecdotes has frequently heard him declare, by this he acquired what knowledge he had of the English language, for of the rules of grammar he was totally ignorant. *

It would be defrauding his memory of a debt due from justice, should I omit to remark that he not only always spoke of his mother's attentions with filial gratitude, but when his situation enabled him to follow the impulse of his mind, made her happiness his first care.+ She lived to see her instructions matured by time, and the public

* I think it is said, that Cowley's school-master could never prevail upon him to learn the rules of grammar; yet, from the prose-writings of Cowley, who that has read them will with-hold praise.

+ This will appear by several letters in this volume.

public diftinguifh and protect what fhe had planted and foftered. -

At about eleven years of age he went to a fchool at Hemel-Hemftead, taught by the late Doctor Stirling, where he did not remain above twelve months, but fhort as the period was, contrived to enlarge his acquaintance with the Englifh claffics, to acquire fome knowledge of French, and learn the common rules of Arithmetic.

From this place he returned to London, and having fhewn an early propenfity to drawing, was placed as a kind of houfe pupil to the late Mr. Fournier, who was then a Drawing-Mafter, a man poffeffed of great verfatility of talent, but deftitute of that prudence which might have rendered his abilities ufeful to himfelf or family.*

-

* Fournier's conduct, or rather want of conduct, feems to have been very fimilar to what the Duke of Buckingham's

From a perfon of this defcription it is not to be fuppofed young Henderfon could obtain

Buckingham's would probably have been, had his Grace ranked with plebeians.   Fournier was,

> " In the courfe of one revolving moon,
> " Engraver, painter, fidler, and buffoon."

His grand ambition was being able to do what any other man could, and having a happy facility, in the courfe of a few years he diftinguifhed himfelf as an engraver, painter, mufician, carver, modeller in wax, and teacher of drawing and perfpective, with which he was fo well acquainted as to compofe a book on the fubject, upon the principle of Doctor Brooke Taylor, which has confiderable merit.   In the firft edition, is an etching from an early defign of Mr. Gainfborough's, which Henderfon told me was etched by himfelf, without any affiftance from his mafter.

If we try Fournier by Mr. Bofwell's definition of man, he will be found to have had fome merit.   He

was

obtain many advantages. He was indeed very ill ufed. Part of his employment

was

was a " *cooking animal* † ;" he dreft and fold àlamode beef ; and I am told, that the truffles and morrels which he ufed in making up this compofition, led him to the ftudy of natural hiftory. At one period of his life he kept a chandler's fhop, and could metamorphofe a fprat into an anchovy, fubftitute dried willow leaves for tea, and mix fine fand with his Lifbon fugar ; he was a good carver, a tolerable button-maker, and, I was near faying, not a contemptible buffoon ; but with the utmoft fub-miffion to thofe ingenious gentlemen, who excel in imitating the noife a horfe makes when he is drinking, the purring of a cat, braying of an afs, croaking of a raven, or lowing of a cow ; fuch qualifications would have entitled him to no higher a clafs than, *an imitating*

animal,

---

† The beafts, have memory, judgement, and all the faculties and paffions of our mind, in a certain degree ; but no beaft is a cook.

was to drive his master in a one horse chaise to some academies where he taught, in the neighbourhood of London, and to feed and rub down the horse, on his return to it.

During his stay with Fournier he made a pen and ink drawing from a print of a fisherman smoking his pipe, with sundry accompaniments

animal, rather more cunning than a monkey, and rather more active than an oyster; but Fournier would bear the test of Dr. Franklin's definition. He was a *tool-making animal*‡; he made gravers, and modelling instruments.

When we consider the number of professions he attempted, can we wonder that he did not attain very great excellence in any?

‡ No animal but man makes a thing, by means of which he can make another thing.

accompaniments in the ftile of Teniers. This, as the production of a boy under fourteen years of age, obtained him the honour of the fecond premium from the fociety for the encouragement of arts, and the ftile in which it was executed fhews an accuracy of eye, and power of imitation, very rarely the lot of one fo young.

As this boyifh production was higher in my eftimation than his own, in the infancy of our friendfhip he gave it me, but as it was the only fpecimen of his drawing, I prefented it to Mrs. Henderfon on her marriage, and am informed it is now in the collection of Sir John Elliot.

Soon after this time he came to live with Mr. Cripps, a working filverfmith in St. James's-ftreet, to whom his mother was related, and her intention was that he

fhould

fhould learn that trade, but the death of Mr. Cripps put an end to this fcheme, and he was left at about twenty years of age with very few connections, and without any determinate purfuit.

His only refource feemed to be that of becoming an affiftant in a filverfmith's fhop, but even this fituation, humble as it may feem, was not very eafy to obtain ; for, on application to a perfon of the trade, the higheft terms offered were twenty-five pounds a year. A propofal was foon after made him to become out-door clerk to a banker, upon a falary little better than the foregoing. Both thefe offers he communicated to a friend, who warmly oppofed his accepting terms fo very inferior to what his abilities ought to command, and advifed him to turn his attention to the ftage, for which he thought him eminently qualified; but Hen-

derfon

derfon hefitated at this advice, declaring his circumftance did not enable him to wait the tedious delays of managers. Being, however, affured, that he might confider the houfe, intereft, and purfe of his friend, at his fervice, until he was fituated to his own fatisfaction, he directed his endeavours to an introduction amongft the *Dramatis Perfonæ*; endeavours in which he encountered difficulties, delays, and mortifications, which cannot be conceived by thofe who have not been in fimilar fituations; which would have abated the vigour of purfuit, and cooled the ardour of expectation in almoft any other man; but he feems to have poffeffed, even at that time, a confcioufnefs of talents that when feen, would force themfelves into notice, and when noticed muft be encouraged.

He

He however paffed his time eafily and chearfully, in the fociety of a family where he was treated with all the attention that friendfhip could prompt, by whom his intereft was confidered as connected with their own, who fincerely efteemed him, were pleafed with his talents, and gratified by his pleafantry; and perhaps it would not have been eafy to point out a man who poffeffed fuch convivial powers as he did in the younger part of his life. His obfervation was quick, his comprehenfion ample, his manners moft lively and conciliating; but the ludicrous light in which he faw and frequently exhibited any object that prefented itfelf, created him enemies, who, though they were pleafed with his wit had no great reiifh for his fatire, when exercifed upon themfelves*.

---

* A city dealer in little trinkets, whofe ever fmiling face bears fome refemblance to Lord Monboddo's

The Ode to the memory of Shakefpeare being at this time popular, Henderfon attempted

Aborigine, became ambitious of being enrolled an artift in an exhibition catalogue, made a copy of the Duke of Leinfter's arms in *human hair,* and brought it for Mr. Henderfon's approbation, telling him he wifhed a *pat* infcription written under, that it might be noticed in the exhibition room. " Sir, (fays Henderfon) I will give you one, that had you known and confidered the advice of the Delphic oracle, you would have chofen for yourfelf: it fhall be allufive." " Thank you, Sir," fays the other.—" You obferve, (continued Henderfon) the fupporters are two monkies rampant, proper, and very pretty they are indeed ; lend me a pen, Sir, and I will write you an infcription from the great Milton. Here it is : read it aloud, Sir."

———— " *In their looks divine,*
" *The image of their glorious Maker fhone.*"

Happening to fee a manufcript, which one of his friends was preparing for the prefs, entitled, " Original

C   Tales

tempted it in Mr. Garrick's manner, and with fuch fuccefs, that it muft have been a very accurate ear which could diftinguifh one fpeaker from the other*.

Some of the confequences which refulted from this talent, he defcribes in the following letter to a young divine:

Tales for the Inftruction of Young Gentlemen and Ladies," he infcribed in the title page the following quotation:

" T A L E S!

" *Told by an idiot, full of found and fury,*
" *Signifying nothing."*

The book was not publifhed.

* His firft public exhibition was in a barn, or fome fuch place, at the polite village of Iflington, where he recited the Ode for the benefit of a few unfortunates, who called themfelves a company of comedians.

One of the audience, who had retired from the plains of Devonfhire to breathe the pure air of Iflington, in his

later

London, 1st Jan. 1770.

To the Reverend Mr. P——.

I Find T—— has written to you. I suppose you will correspond with him. He sent me his farce with a message, begging me to offer it to Dibden, which I have declined, as thinking it more proper*er* to present it either to Garrick or Colman. I wish it may answer his expectations. Does not a wish sometimes imply a doubt.——
* * * * * * * and I sat in judgement upon it the other night, and brought in our verdict—*Ignoramus.*

I am glad you told me of the thirty manuscript sermons, I should else have rose

C 2

early,

later years, declared he was certain, the speaker *must be,* either Mr. Garrick, or Antichrist.

early, and late took reſt, to tranſlate Flechier's and Bourdalon's for you. L——
thinks you are dead; for aſking me how you
did, I replied, you ſlept with your fathers, I
made him happy by telling him it was a me-
taphorical ſleep, and that you would awake
a profound theologiſt.

It was a very raſh propoſal I made to you
of commenting upon authors. I thought it
might have been done, but when I go about
it I feel myſelf ſtrangely confined in my
powers, like thoſe who do not apprehend the
danger of a precipice till they are on the
brink. I think I will give up the thought
'till you are more at leiſure. R—— I ſeldom ſee. L——— never. Thoſe hours
I am not with I——— are paſſed in
drinking, and writing ſerious reflections on,
and bitter invectives againſt, drunkenneſs,
both in verſe and proſe. If this contra-

riety continues, and heaven only knows how long it may continue, you may expect a fatire againft fornication written from Marjoram's.——Is not this in your language the character of one *buffeted by Satan?* B——, in the fimplicity of his heart told me, one day, after much bewailing the reduction of his circumftances, " that it was a great mercy he had not *taken* to drinking," feeling himfelf, I fuppofe, totally unable to refift any impulfe which it fhould pleafe Lucifer to embarrafs him with. I faw your letter to E——, wherein I ftand recorded as a fool for quoting Macbeth upon fuch a fubject as your lazinefs—and this is owing to my modefty, that would rather talk in other people's words than my own. But

" Hence ye vain fears of criticifm, hence,
By caution nurs'd, at happinefs' expence ;

To

> To prove my pen in trite quotations run,
> Thine own the quibble, and thine own the pun;
> 'Take thine full swing, and in the critic's spite,
> If nonsense urge thee, freely nonsense write."

I will make you repent the reproof, for talk I must—and if it is all my own. But you have brought it upon yourself, and so are less to be pitied. E—— writes with me. His will be a good letter, and I am glad I have found the way of diverting your indignation. He will put you into spirits, and you will read mine with better temper.

I wish we could form a triumvirate at T——'s; he has written me a very genteel and pressing invitation. I have traces upon my memory of much happiness with him, and it was a happiness that I like, independent of auxiliary hogsheads. There is a natural festivity in him that will always entertain,

entertain, and I have known him ftart much excellent wit and good-natured fatire. I believe matrimony draws off a man's genius ; his letters to me are not near fo pleafant, nor fo brilliant as they were wont to be. I fuppofe you will rebuke me for that metaphor, and therefore you may erafe *genius, and infert attention,* which is the fame thing with thofe like you, with whom defire is power.

There is a burlefque parody of Garrick's Ode publifhed, on Le Stue, cook to the Duke of Newcaftle, and teftimonies to his genius and merit prefixed.

I wifh Garrick's had been ftill at the bottom of Avon, from whence I am fure he fifhed up fome of it ; for it has ruined my conftitution in fpeaking it. I have been up till three in the morning, four nights a

week,

week, for this month paſt. Inſtead of ſleep, I get flattery; and inſtead of dreaming of Miſs ————, claret.

I wiſh I could convey to you a few ſounds which the boobies about me ſay are exceedingly like Garrick's, but they would have no melody mixed with the poſtman's horn. If I could get a cake of Rabelais' ice, in which to mix them, they would thaw by your veſtry fire, and give you ſome idea of London flummery. But our air is not intenſe enough to make ſuch a cake; therefore you muſt take it on my word, that I am flattered, inebriated, ſpoiled—Yet, as a *bon vivant* I owe it ſomething, for it has brought me acquainted with diſhes I never before heard off—wines I never before taſted—and fruit I never before ſaw, except through the fruiterer's windows.—I eat pine-apple the other day, and if

that

that be the fruit the Devil offered Eve, I don't fee how fhe could refift it.——Otway has dealt a little unfair in his bitter invective againft women——

" And for an apple damn'd mankind."

He fhould have added that it was a pineapple ; with all my dramatick faith, I never could believe it was worth her while to tranfgrefs for a mere apple, even though it had been a nonpareil.

S H A N D Y.

At

At this time he belonged to an evening society, confifting of about twelve or fourteen members, who wifhed to unite to the feftivity of Anacreon, the humour of Prior, the harmony of Pope; and, above all, the fenfibility and pleafantry of Sterne*.

Part of the plan of this club, who met at a houfe in Maiden-lane once a week, was, to fubftitute fome toaft, in the place of a health to the political idol of the day, or the premier of the month, about whofe real principles their different partizans are fometimes a little in the dark, and whofe very names are the roots from whence fpring up difputes,

" About it, goddefs, and about it."

that

* The name they adopted was the Shandean fociety.

that do not much tend to inform, or enliven the unfortunate hearers, and frequently end in

"   Contention fierce, endleſs debate, and hate irreconcileable."

To avoid which evils, it was a rule, that when the ſociety meet, the Preſident pour a libation, and drink to the memory of ſome departed genius, with whoſe merits every perſon preſent either was, or might be acquainted, under the denomination of a SKULL; after which, the next man gave a *ſentiment*, and the next a *ſkull*. If for inſtance, they had drank the memory of Shakeſpeare, it was expected that he who was next in progreſſion, ſhould give a ſentiment, which ſhould have ſome alluſion to the bard, or his writings, *and be new*. One equally appoſite, was, to follow the names

of

of Rabelais, Cervantes, or Sterne. But, alas! it was foon found that fuch a rapid fucceffion of fkulls to fentiments, and fentiments to fkulls, promoted fo quick a circulation of the glafs, as to clafh with part of the plan of the inftitution, which was to go home tolerably fober*.

To correct this inconvenience, it was ordained in council, that each member fhould bring with him a volume of his favourite writer, and read fuch part aloud as he thought would moft contribute to the amufement of the fociety. Henderfon produced a volume of Sterne, the god of his idolatry, entered

* It was obferved by a theatrical veteran, who fometimes honoured this fociety with a vifit, that " though it was a very pleafant and chearful thing to get drunk, it was a very difagreeable bufinefs to get fober."

entered fo fully into the fpirit of his author, fo happily difcriminated the characters, and fo forcibly exhibited them, that his companions finding more gratification in hearing him than themfelves, which I believe will be acknowledged as ftrong a teftimony of approbation as could be given by a fociety compofed of reading men, conftituted him reader to the club, and without an act of parliament, confirmed his right to a name which had been given him by a friend a fhort time before; decreeing that from, and after that time, he fhould be diftinguifhed by the name of SHANDY, an appellation he retained many years.

The manner in which he read Sterne's works, threw new light upon many paf-

fages,

fages†, and was the fource of much in-formation as well as pleafantry. In the humorous paffages it called forth flafhes of merriment, and drew tears from every eye in the pathetic. Never fhall I forget the effect he gave to the ftory of Le Fevre. It kindled a fiame of admiration, and pro-moted a propofal to devote a day to the memory of the author, pour a libation over his grave, and fpeak a requiem to his de-parted fpirit*.

This

---

† It was firft obferved in this fociety, that until the appearance of the four afterifks (* * * *) with which Sterne has fo frequently embellifhed his volumes, the two following lines were totally mifconceived:

———— " If weak women go aftray,

" Their *ftars* are more in fault than they."

* A rainy day prevented the full completion of the plan.

This was the determination of a moment, and affented to with enthufiaftic eagernefs. Shandy was appointed to felect what he thought moft fit for the occafion, and the next week produced an Ode, on which the candid critic will look with fome allowance, when he confiders it as the hafty production of a man little more than twenty years of age. The ardour with which the fubject is treated, will, I hope, be confidered as an adequate apology for the inaccuracies in fome of the lines.

The occafion of its being written, the idolatry with which the name of Sterne was venerated by the company who attended the recital, and, above all, the energy, and pa-

thetic

plan. The Ode was, therefore, read to a felect party in a private houfe.

thetic feeling which was difplayed by the
fpeaker, gave it a moft powerful effect,
and it has furely too much merit to be
buried in oblivion.

O D E.

INTENDED TO HAVE BEEN SPOKEN AT THE TOMB
OF THE LATE LAWRENCE STERNE,
ON HIS BIRTH DAY.

T H I S day be facred,—let no hoftile found,
Prophane the honours deftin'd to his fhade,
Hence ye unhallow'd from this votive ground,
No gueft improper on our rites pervade.
Before his name let wanton fatire fly,
The ftoic's rancour melt before his beams,
Let fpleen avoid the lightning of his eye,
And fink for fhelter in oblivion's ftreams.
Hence too, unfeeling and cold blooded gueft,
Dull ignorance, in folemn garments dreft.

But come thou Goddefs fair and free,
On earth y'clep'd Philanthropy,
Fill our bofoms, crown our board
With all thy fpirit can afford.
Thy fon, thy elder born we fing,
Sound the hautboys, tune the ftring,

D   Need'ft

Need'ft thou, goddefs, need'ft thou learn,
All our notes are rais'd to Sterne.
To him our grateful notes afcend,
Him we folicit to attend.

If 'midft the fpheres,
Tun'd by the bright angelic choir,
Thy fpirit hears
The tribute of a mortal lyre,
Deign, oh deign to fhed thy power,
Thy mighty magic on this feftive hour.
Nor, when my grateful verfe reveals,
What every fon of candour feels,
Let thy gentle foul difdain,
What alive had given thee pain ;
Our motives thou may'ft try above,
And know our praife the tribute of our love.

Shame to the man, and to his memory fhame,
Whofe tongue licentious robs thee of thy fame.
Oh hadft thou liv'd when critics learn'd and wife,
To juftice faithful, own'd no other ties ;
Dupes to no party, and no flaves to fear,
In fentence candid, yet in judgment clear,

Feeling

Feeling like men, like men their fentence own'd
Nor honour'd dullnefs, though by dunces thron'd,
Then had thy facred buft in triumph rofe,
And twining laurel fcreen'd thee from thy foes.
But he unhappy fell on evil days,
When *barren* fentiment ufurp'd his praife.
When folly bore the honours and the crown,
Which fhould have deck'd his temples with renown.
When he from virtue greateft honour drew,
And held philanthropy to public view,
Adorn'd with all that can fecure efteem,
The monarch's glory, and the poet's theme,
That balm of blood and confidence of mind,
Impell'd to pity, to fufpicion blind,
That bofom, open to each focial claim,
In virtue ardent, negligent of fame;
That heart, unable to repel relief,
In courage manly, feminine in grief.
In pleafure, harmlefs, innocent, and mild,
Warm as a man, forgiving as a child,
Ev'n then they dar'd to violate his page;
In virtue barren, fruitful in their rage,
Vex'd, inly vex'd, that on infpection clear,
They fearch'd their hearts and found no Toby there.

D 2

Stung

Stung, inly stung, they snatch'd the pen,
And told the tasteless sons of men,
That he whose spirits warm and full,
Could charm the gay, and wake the dull,
Could fix a smile on sorrow's brow,
And steal his grief he knew not how.
Could give new courage to the brave,
And bid his fame survive the grave, .
Could give religion fresher charms,
And lead the stoic to her arms,
Could bid, on touching fancy's string,
Profusion in a desart spring,
Benign vibrations stir the trees,
And chearful rapture swell the breeze,
That he, with all these powers fraught,
Was loose in language, and impure in thought;
Believing virtue, their 'monition took,
And thank'd his stars he had not read the book.

 The idle crew,
 Who never knew
More than these mighty critics chose,
 Soon caught the sound,
 And echoed round,
The friends of Sterne were virtue's foes;

Error

Error confirm'd, what malice had begun,
Till fool and critic, loft their name in one.

Some there arofe who fpurn'd the flavifh tie,
And if they cenfur'd, would at leaft know why;
But all too indolent, or all too dull,
His fruits to gather, or his flowers to cull,
    The loofer parts
    Attach'd their hearts,
But when they hop'd fome grofs defect to clafp,
His wit, like Mercury, efcap'd their grafp.

If high in blood, voluptuous in thought,
Some beam of beauty's emanative fire,
As fwift the meteor glided by he caught,
    It play'd perhaps around his heart,
    But urg'd not foul defire.
    Some kindred tendernefs it warm'd,
    Which ftraight to other themes he drew,
    No longer virtue ftood alarm'd,
But join'd his paffage as he upward flew.
Too weak of wing, or impotent of fight,
Thefe readers loft him in the daring flight:
Thus envy ftung, or dullnefs veil'd his worth,
'Till nature, warm and zealous in his caufe,

Snatch'd

Snatch'd him at once from this ill-judging earth,
To realms where angels hail'd him with applauſe.
Cervantes gaily grave, with accent ſweet,
And laughing Rabelais led him to his feat ;
Yorick, in flaſhes of wild tranſport roar'd,
As when in Denmark's court he ſhook the board.
The ſocial ſhades of tenderneſs and love,
Spread the glad tidings through the courts above.

 All heard, all flew on wings of joy,
 And welcom'd him to peace ſincere,
 To bliſs whoſe raptures never cloy,
 And happineſs unknown to fear.

To us belongs to vindicate his fame,
To pluck the nettle from his ſacred grave,
To turn the darts of malice from their aim,
And point his virtues to the good and brave ;
Nor this a taſk which indolence would ſhun,
'Tis half-accompliſh'd when 'tis once begun ;
Obvious and full they ſtrike upon the ſight,
Nor aſk aſſiſtance from collected light.

Oh !

Oh ! when ye hear his memory defam'd,
His wit misconstrued, or his heart bely'd,
Loud be his warm benevolence proclaim'd,
'Till rage and error blushing turn aside.
Whate'er their motive, ignorance, or whim,
They slander'd nature when they slander'd him.

For me, I own, with grateful transport mov'd,
I love his memory, as the man I lov'd.
Dear to my eye, but dearer to my heart,
Ne'er felt my soul more agonizing smart,
Than when that spirit from its bondage fled,
And gave a second Yorick to the dead.

Besides

Befides Sterne's works, he fometimes read felect paffages from Milton, Pope, Prior, Swift, Gray, and Junius.

The verfification of Pope was too fmooth for him, the fame found fo perpetually recurring upon the fame fyllable, gave a flatnefs which fatigued the ear. The meafure became vapid and lifelefs. From this cenfure I except his manner of reading the Dunciad, to which he gave the full force of its fatire.

Gray's Elegy he always miftook; by endeavouring to exprefs energy, he deftroyed that plaintive folemnity which is furely its peculiar characteriftic. Indeed, the fpecies of poetry in which this Elegy claims the firft place, did not feem to be his *forte*. If he attempted the pathetic it became a whine, and his ear being too correct to

bear

bear the founds of his own voice, he changed his tones, and quitted his author's manner, preferring impropriety to diffonance. In the light airy tales of Prior, where laughing whimficallity is the predominant feature, he was on his proper ground. To "the manly vigour of one fterling line" of Churchill, he added a thoufand beauties. Junius, he efteemed the moft perfect model of Englifh profe, and although unacquainted with the politics of the day, gave full effect to every fentence of that moft fplendid writer. Paradife Loft he deemed a dramatic poem; ftrongly varied the different manners of Moloch, Belial, and the other fallen angels, and entering with fublime energy into the fpirit of the various characters, became, as was faid of his author, as a chariot-wheel wrought into a blaze by its own motion. It was grand, forcible, terrific.

But

But his talents as a reader are so well known from the specimens he exhibited at Freemasons-Hall, that it becomes unnecessary to expatiate upon them here. I am not afraid to aver, and it is an opinion grounded upon some reflection, that he read better in Maiden-lane than he did in Queen-street : he was less theatrical, and more chaste.

It is not very usual for the Dramatis Personæ to distinguish between acting, reciting, and reading ; when reading they attempt to act, and imitate the passions which they are only required to enumerate.

In reading a letter to an audience, they do not always think it necessary to change their intonation. It is *acted*, and uttered with all the buskined pomp of heroic emphasis. Of this error Henderson was never guilty.

Mr.

Mr. Garrick was, I believe, efteemed to have approached very near perfection in playing, that he was above mediocrity in reciting or reading, no man will, I think, affert, who has heard him read, or recite his Jubilee Ode.

The great requifites neceffary to conftitute a reader, feem to be, a good ear, a voice capable of inflexion, an underftanding of, and tafte for, the beauties of the author, and a feeling, an ardour, an enthufiafm, which will warm the mind to difplay them; to all this muft be added a judgment that will guard againft extremes. Whether Mr. Henderfon was, or was not, in poffeffion of *all* thefe requifites, is a queftion I will not prefume to decide. I think he read better than any man I ever heard.

Ho

He ufed to fport an opinion, that the great difference of reading confifted in under-ftanding, or not underftanding, the author's meaning. I mentioned inftances where men had written with great knowledge of their fubject, and expreffed their fentiments in glowing and brilliant colours, who yet fo totally mangled and weakened their own works when they attempted to read them, as to obfcure the brighteft paffages, and dif-guife the moft obvious fentences. " Sir, faid he, reft affured, they did not fully under-ftand what they read. Some men have a trick of ftringing words together, fo as to impofe upon the underftanding, but they do not wholly conceive what they are about. Let any one be fully and powerfully im-preffed with an author's meaning, and if his voice and articulation are not defective, he cannot fail impreffing that meaning upon his hearers. A female mendicant under-
ftands

ftands what fhe wants, and therefore her
entreaties are uttered in the tones beft calculated to reach the heart, and with an emphafis that rarely offends the ear. A tho-
roughly enraged fcold is infinitely more
pointed in her oratory, than is a gentleman
in a wig and band at Weftminfter-hall.

" She is animated from conceiving her
fubject, and feeling the paffion, fhe re-
prefents it. An infant is perfect mafter
of the art of fupplication before he can
fpeak, and when he attains that power
never afks for any thing with an improper emphafis until he is *taught* to read,
when he is harraffed about points, confounded by a multitude of inftructions,
and fent to a *Demofthenes maker*, who
gives him rules for utterance, and modes
of fpeech, and a *manner* of delivery, that
enables the well inftructed young gentleman

man to torture the ears of all within compass of his voice, whether he is doomed
to exhibit in the pulpit, or the senate, at
the bar, or upon the stage. The human
voice is in a great degree artificial, and
whatever any one chuses to make it. You
find general similarity in the tones of people of one profession. One set of tones
are appropriated to the bar, another to
the pulpit. I have heard that most su-
blime composition, the burial service, slo-
vened over in such a manner that I could
scarcely understand two words in a sentence,
and yet the voice has had a kind of solemn sound, a pious noise, that has given
great effect.

" Sounds have infinite power without words.
This should seem to extend to music, but
with me it does not. I have little gratification from what I am told is exquisite.
Some

Some one fays, it is become the art of exe-
cuting difficulties. It was a good wifh,
would to heaven thefe *difficulties* were *im-
poffibilities.*

" When I recited Mr. Garrick's Ode in a
private room, I felt what I faid, and I
believe gave it fome effect. Very different was it upon the ftage. My feelings
were weakened and confounded by the band,
my voice loft its fcale, and was overpower-
ed by the mufic in the orcheftra."

This, it muft be acknowledged is a
rhapfody, and as fuch was fpoken, but
there are fome truths in it.

Mr. Pope exhibited an inftance, that a
man may have the moft delicate ear for
the harmony of numbers, and yet have no
fort of tafte for the harmony of founds.

Swift

Swift is another example, and I am inclined to fufpect from Mr. Garrick's manner of finging, that he had not, whatever
he might chufe to profefs, much knowledge of, or tafte in, mufic.

Would it be fuppofed from the meafured,
harmony of Dr. Johnfon's periods, that he
had fcarcely any perception of it. He knew
a drum from a trumpet, and a bagpipe from
a guittar, which he owned was about the
extent of his knowledge in mufic*.

Mr. Henderfon had great delight in pe-
rufing books that abounded in the marvel-
lous. Sir John Mandeville's Travels, Pontoppidan's Norway, Peter Wilkins' Voyage
to the Moon, or Wanley's Wonders of the

Little

* Bofwell's Journal, 1ft edition, page 363.

Little World were *in deliciis.** With equal eagerneſs he ſought for and read the ac-
counts

* We ſay *Noſcitur a Socio*—May we not, with equal truth, ſay, *Noſcitur a Libris.*

A knowledge of the particular ſpecies of books which attract men of genius and ſtudy in their hours of deſultory reading, would be curious and worth ſpeculation : ſuch knowledge might ſometimes enable us to develope the bias of their characters with more truth than do their graveſt biographers.

For the gratification of the curious I have ſubjoined the titles of a few books in Mr. Henderſon's ſtudy, in ſome of which the ludicrous and the horrible, " for maſterſhippe do ſtrive."—The lamentable and true Tragedie of Maiſter Arden of Feverſham, who was moſte wickedlie murdered by means of his wantonne Wife, who hired two deſperate Ruffians, Blacke Will and Shakbagge, to kill him.   Life and Death of Lewis Gaufredy, with his abominable Sorceries, after ſelling himſelf to the Devil.   A bloody Newe Yeares Gifte.   A

E

counts of murders, battles, maſſacres, mar-
tyrdoms, earthquakes, the death of Regulus,

true Declaration of the cruel and moſt bloody Murther
of Maiſter Robert Heath, In his own houſe at High
Holborne, being the ſigne of the Fire Brande. A true
Relation how a Woman at Atherbury having uſed divers
horrid Imprecations, was ſuddainlie burned to Aſhes,
there being no Fire neare her. Helliſh Murder com-
mitted by a French Midwife. Hiſtories of Apparitions,
Spirits, Viſions, and other wonderful Illuſions of the
Devil. The Surey Demoniac, or Satan, his dreadful
Judgements upon Richard Dugdale. A Pleaſaunte
Treatiſe of Witches, their Impes and Meetings. Newes
from Italie, or a moſt lamentable Tragedie lately be-
fallen. *Phyloſithie,* wherein outlandiſh Birds, Beaſts,
and Fiſhes, are taught to ſpeak Engliſh. Tarquatus
Vandermer, his ſeven Yeares Studie in the Arte offe
Magicke upon the twelve Monthes of the Yeare. The
Devil Conjured, by Thomas Lodge: a Diſcourſe of
the ſottille Practiſes of Divelles by Witches. The
Miſeries of inforſt Marriage. Lavaterus of Ghoſtes
and Spirits walking by Night, and of ſtraunge Noyſes,
Crackes,

gulus*, or burning of Cranmer, particulars of
a criminal's behaviour when broken upon the
wheel,

Crackes, *and so forths*. Baylie, his Wall Flower, as
it grew out of the stone Chamber in Newgate. Ad-
mirable Historie of a Magician, who seduced a pious
Womanne to be a Witch. And though last, not least
in Love, King James, his Dæmonologiæ.

* A writer of the last century has thrown this lamentable story into a most ludicrous point of view. I
believe the lines are not generally known : perhaps it
will be said they are not worth knowing ; however here
they are :—

When the bold Carthaginian,
Fought with Rome for dominion,
    Little Reg was ta'en in the strife ;
When his eye-lids they par'd,
Good Lord how he star'd,
    And could not go sleep for his life.

When

wheel, the barbarities Cortes and other zealous propagators of the gospel inflicted upon the Indians, the tortures suffered by the victims of superstition in the Inquisition, or any event whether in, or out of nature, which was calculated to give strong and forcible impressions.*

By

When the bold Carthaginian,
Fought with Rome for dominion,
   Little Reg was ta'en in the quarrel,
So they took him up a hill,
And sore against his will,
   They trundled him down in a barrel.

To those idolaters of ancient patriotism, and ancient history, to whom this description may appear a shocking insult on the memory of so celebrated a hero, it may be a consolation to recollect, that the best critics and commentators, have esteemed the whole story of the death of Regulus, to be a fiction.

* If it should be inferred from hence that his disposition was cruel, the inference would be unjust.

Mortimer,

By the perufal of fuch books as thefe,
objects of terror became familiar to his
mind,

Mortimer, the hiftorical painter, in whom were united
the favage grandeur of Salvator Rofa, and the terrific
graces of Spagnolette ; who, joined to a fublimity of
idea, and accuracy of delineation, not exceeded by Mi-
chael Angelo, a delicacy of pencil equal to Teniers ;
was moft happy, and, I think moft fuccefsful, when
fketching, or painting objects, from which the common
eye withdrew. His four paintings of the progrefs of
vice, in the very well chofen collection of Doctor Bates,
of Miffenden, is one example of this truth.

From hints in Fox's Book of Martyrs, he made a
number of moft fpirited fketches, in which are reprefented the fufferings of men, women, and children.
Scorching their hands with lighted tapers, burning their
eyes out with hot irons, and the whole exhibition of the
ufes made of thofe powerful engines of argument, the
whips, hooks, racks ; but, above all, the *thumb vice*, by
which unbelievers are fcrewed up to the proper faith.

Yet,

mind, and perhaps enabled him to exhibit with such warmth of colouring, portraits

Yet, with this disposition for contemplating, and displaying such objects, Mortimer had a soul, "Open as day to melting charity, a tear for pity," and a heart the most susceptible of tender impressions. He made the kindest allowances for the errors of others, and would not have trod upon the poor beetle. When he erred, and who shall dare to name any man as faultless? his errors had their root in virtues which the generous warmth of his heart carried to excess. Added to all this, he had an hilarity that brightened every eye, and gladdened every heart. I knew his mind well, but that knowledge should have deterred me from attempting to describe it, had I considered that Sterne has so exactly delineated the leading features by which it was actuated, in the benevolence and sensibility of character which distinguished his uncle Toby.

In the society of Mortimer I passed some of the happiest years of my life, and the remembrance of the very intimate, brotherly, and unbroken friendship with which

traits of Shakefpeare's moſt terrific characters, from which ſpirits of a more
exquiſite texture, unaccuſtomed to the
contemplation of ſuch objects, would
ſhrink with horror. For I believe thoſe
who have hearts of ſuch fuſceptibility as
to receive impreſſions of joy, love, or
grief, in an extreme degree, are by no
means the moſt eminently qualified for
communicating thoſe impreſſions to an
audience. A man whoſe feelings are ſo
alive as to overbalance the difproportionate
ſtrength of his mind, becomes liable to
be awed into forgetfulneſs, the paſſions are
overwhelmed in a ſtorm of their own

E 4

raiſing,

we were united until his death, affords me one of thoſe
melancholy pleaſures which may be felt, but cannot be
deſcribed—A tear drops at the recollection. The loſs
of ſuch a friend leaves a chaſm in one's life and happineſs, which is very, very, rarely filled up.

raiſing, and the actor drowned in a deluge of his own tears. The mind wrought up to real tenderneſs, loſes, in ſome meaſure, the power of expreſſing that which is fictitious, and exceſs of ſenſibility defeats its own purpoſe. *   There is a point to which the paſſions muſt be raiſed, to diſplay that exhibition of them which ſcatters contagious

* This may be thought at firſt ſight to claſh with the maxim of Horace; but, maturely conſidered, may perhaps be found nearly to coincide with it.

I am told this is not the philoſophy of the green-room, notwithſtanding which, I ſuſpect the contrary opinion to be the philoſophy of the diſtaff. To ſay, though with the utmoſt dramatic dignity of emphaſis,

" *He, muſt, have, feeling, who, makes, others, feel;*"

May be replied to by,

" *Who drives fat oxen, ſhould himſelf be fat.*"

gious tenderneſs through the whole Theatre, but carried, " though but the breadth of
a hair," beyond that point, the picture
becomes an overcharged carricature, as
likely to create laughter, as diffuſe diſtreſs.
There is a certain *term* in the mind which
is exactly proportionate to produce ſympa-
thy, *beyond* which limit, or *within* it, the
effect ceaſes to be produced. *

The

* It is a general opinion, that a good player muſt
have a ſound judgment, and conceive his author's
meaning before he can expreſs it ; yet I have ſeen inſtances where nature having denied an underſtanding,
has kindly given what did well enough as a ſubſtitute,
and paſſed muſter before an audience very decently.
Theſe inſtances, indeed, were many years ago—I believe ;—but, inſtead of an opinion, I venture an anecdote, and let the gentle reader draw his own con-
cluſion.

The power of mimickry which Henderfon poffeffed in a moft eminent degree,
and

When the late Mr. Reddifh's indifpofition of mind
rendered him incapable of fulfilling his duties at the
Theatre, and he was by his inability reduced from a falary of twelve or fourteen pounds a week, to an income
of feventy pounds a year from the fund, fome of his
friends made intereft with the manager to grant him
a benefit. The play advertifed was Cymbeline, and
Mr. Reddifh was announced for Pofthumus. He
was to pafs an hour previous to his performance at a
houfe where I was afked to meet him. He came into
the room with the ftep of an ideot, his eye wandering
and his whole countenance vacant. I congratulated
him on his being enough recovered to perform. Yes,
fir, replied he, I fhall perform, and in the garden fcene
I fhall aftonifh you!—In the garden fcene, Mr. Reddifh?——I thought you were to play Pofthumus.—
No, fir, I play Romeo.—My good man, faid the gentleman of the houfe, you play Pofthumus. Do I, replied he; I am forry for it. However what muft be,
muft be. At the time appointed he fet out for the
Theatre.

and exercised with that indiscriminate negligent sportiveness, which meaning no

.   evil,

Theatre. The gentleman who went with him, for he
was not capable of walking without a guide, told me
that his mind was so imprest with the character of Romeo, he was reciting it all the way, and when he came
into the green-room it was with extreme difficulty they
could persuade him he was to play any other part.
That when the time came for his appearance, they
pushed him on the stage, fearing he would begin
with a speech of Romeo. With the same expectation
I stood in the pit close to the orchestra, and being so
near had a perfect view of his face. The instant he
came in sight of the audience his recollection seemed
to return, his countenance resumed meaning, his eye
appeared lighted up, he made the bow of modest respect, and went through the scene much better than
I had ever before seen him. On his return to the
green-room, the image of Romeo returned to his mind,
nor did he lose it until his second appearance, when the
moment he had the *cue*, he went through the scene, and
in this weak and *imbecile* state of his understanding,
performed

evil, feared no confequences, was the fource of fome inconveniences, which led him to repent having difplayed it in the unguarded manner he frequently did.

Mr.

performed the whole better than I ever faw him before, and it was a character in which I had feen him often, and never contemptible. But he appeared to much greater advantage then, than when he had the full exercife of his reafon. His manner was lefs affuming, and more natural. After that time he never performed.

It brought to my recollection an anecdote I have heard of his late majefty, who, naming an officer that he intended fhould command in an expedition of fome confequence, was told by the Duke of Newcaftle that " the gentleman was by no means eligible for fo important a ftation, being pofitively mad." "Is he," replied the king," he fhall go for all that, and before he fets out I wifh to my God he would bite fome of my Generals, and make them mad too."

Mr. Garrick was at this time the object of his imitation, and not much gratified with the freedom, nor much difposed to ferve the perfon who took it; under thefe circumftances an introduction to him was difficult, his different friends were therefore fought out and applied to for their intereft. Among other applications, one was made to the late Paul Hiffernan, of dull memory, who was at that time one of the attendants at the managers *levee.*

When the name and intention of Henderfon was announced to Hiffernan, he looked in his face with the utmoft gravity for half a minute, and then, like a drill ferjeant giving the word of command, vociferated " *Pleafe to ftand upon your pins.*"—Henderfon ftood up.—Mr. Hiffernan did the fame.——"Now," fays he, " young

gentleman,

gentleman, I'll soon see if you'll ever make an actor.—I'll soon see whether or not you are fit for the stage." Then stalking with solemn dignity to a table drawer, he opened it, and took out a ball of packthread, from which he first cut off a long piece and tied the knife to the end, by way of plummet, this done marched up to the young candidate, and having first got upon a chair, to be the better able to reach, held the packthread to the top of Henderson's head, and let the knife drop to the ground, by which it was now seen he intended to try how tall he was. This ceremony over he descended, took out of his pocket a two foot rule, and measured the length of the packthread; then putting on a most melancholy countenance, shook his head, and exclaimed, " young gentleman, I am sorry to mortify you, I am very sorry to mortify you,

but

but go your ways home, fet your thoughts upon fomewhat elfe, mind your bufinefs, be it what it will, and remember I tell you, for the fock or bufkin you won't do; —you will not do, fir, by an inch and a quarter."

This muft be acknowledged to be fomewhat in the fpirit of Serjeant Kite, but it was Paul's mode of meafuring the talents of thofe who afpired to the ftage. —*Excellent critic !*"

A theatrical veteran, whofe abilities have been looked up to by the laft age with admiration, and are regarded by the prefent age with aftonifhment; whofe judgment was thought matured by time, and whofe decrees were uttered with that firmnefs and oracular dignity, which confounds if it does not convince, and filences where

it

it cannot confute, was requefted to hear Mr. Henderfon rehearfe, point out his errors, and advife the beft method of improving his recitation. " Sir," fays this Ariftarchus of the drama, " Sir, the young man has genius, but the firft thing he does muft be to *un*learn all that he has already *learned*, until he does that, he cannot *learn* to be a player."

So fevere was the fentence of this Neftor of the green-room, but even this, did not deter the ftage-ftruck hero from his theatrical purfuit, he had the true enthufiaftic ardour which gains ftrength from oppofition; every difcouragement feemed rather to encreafe than abate his eagernefs; and as accefs was not to be had to Mr. Garrick, he endeavoured to obtain an introduction to fome of the other managers. But managers, like minifters of ftate, were

not,

not, he found, very willing to hear, and when they did hear, not very eafy to pleafe.

One objected to him, that never having been upon any ftage, he was unftudied in his parts. Another excellent judge of the Englifh language, that in reading Pope, he made *verfe* of it. A third, that his voice was not ftrong enough for the ftage. A fourth, that his fpeaking was hufky, and his tones too fat.*

F   He,

* His continual imitation of Mr. Garrick's voice, might, in a degree, contribute to give his own a refemblance of it; and that imitation was formed upon tones, which, melodious as they had once been, began to contract the hufkinefs fo commonly attendant upon old age. His fo frequently repeating fpeeches in the manner of Falftaff, gave what the fame critic calls a famefs of tone.

He, however, had friends, who renewed application to Mr. Garrick, and the manager's good underſtanding ſeemed to have vanquiſhed his reſentment, for he heard him rehearſe, ſaid, that his voice had neither ſtrength nor modulation enough for the London ſtage, but adviſed him to try his powers at a country theatre, for the purpoſe of forwarding an introduction to which, he would write to Mr. Palmer, then manager of the Bath company, who gave for anſwer, that he ſhould have an engagement, if approved of by Mr. Keaſeberry, who was then director of a *corps dramatique* at Richmond. Mr. Keaſeberry heard and approved, and, in September, 1772, Mr. John Henderſon was enrolled as one of the Bath comedians for three years.

The firſt year he was to receive one guinea per week; the ſecond, one guinea

and

and a half; and the third year, two guineas. Befides this enormous falary, he was to have an annual benefit.

The object of his ambition attained, he trembled with apprehenfion, doubted if his figure was fufficiently important, queftioned if he was grounded enough in any one character to venture it before the awful tribunal of the public, and could he have protracted his *entrée* for another year, would moft gladly have done it : fo great was his dread of difappointment and difgrace, that he affumed the name of Courtenay, and, under the protection of that name, made his *coup d'effai* at Bath, on the 6th of October, 1772, in the part of *Hamlet*.

The writer of this went with a number of friends from London to Bath, to fee the *debut'* of this young candidate for the dra-

matic

matic laurel, whofe apprehenfions were fo
alive, and whofe fears were fo exceffive, that
it was with difficulty he advanced upon the
ftage, and made his firft bow to the audience. They received him with that indulgence which is fo generally exercifed to a
young performer, and when he fpoke, gave
that ftill refpectful attention, which is perhaps a ftronger teftimony of approbation
than the thundering clapping of a thoufand
hands. But of the gratification which re-
fults from this mode of applaufe, he had a
large portion at the end of each act; and
before the conclufion of the firft, his fears
were fo far difpelled, and his terror fo much
fubfided, that his underftanding recovered
its natural expanfion; and although his
powers had not attained their full maturity,
yet the ftrong traits of judgment he difplayed in conceiving the outline of the part,
the fenfibility and feeling he exhibited

through

through the whole of the performance, the accuracy of his articulation, and the proper modulation of his tones, marked themfelves as diftinctly as they did at any fubfequent period.

In that fiery ordeal for dramatic candidates, Hamlet's advice to the players, he manifefted fo clear a conception of his author, with fo much eafe and propriety of recitation, as difplayed his power of difcrimination, and gave every right to augur the excellence he afterwards attained.*

Old

* When the performance ended, I went into the green-room—Let the reader of extreme delicacy avoid this note; or, if fhe reads it, not accufe me of omitting the proper warning.

Mr.

Old Mr. Giffard, under whofe management Garrick made his firft appearance, and who had been witnefs to the dramatic rife of

Mr. Henderfon's predeceffor, in the character, was *Lee*, who ufed to play it in a fuit of black velvet, much too large for Henderfon ; he was, therefore, under the neceffity of performing it in a fuit of black cloth. Extreme agitation occafioned a perfpiration. The coat was wet as if it had been " immerfed in the ocean." The performance ended, Hamlet refigned his habit to the keeper of the wardrobe, who received it with aftonifhment and horror ; hung it to the fire, lifted up both his hands, and exclaimed, in the true nafal tone of a parifh clerk, " Heaven blefs us all ! what a forry fight is here : 'twas the Lord's mercy he did not play it in the black velvet——it would have raifed all the pile. They may talk of Mufter Lee, and Mufter Lee, and Mufter Lee, but Mufter Lee is nothing to this man—for what they call perfpiration." A perfon prefent obferved, that the fevereft critics muft acknowledge the young gentleman had played the character with great warmth, if not with fpirit.

of many of the moſt diſtinguiſhed actors. Who, in the courſe of a long life, had ſeen the dawnings and progreſſive exertions, of numbers whoſe abilities had been ſanctioned by public approbation ; Mr. Giffard thought his talents of the firſt magnitude, deſired to be gratified by a morning's rehearſal upon the ſtage, when, with the ſpirit of prophecy, the old man foretold the future eminence of the young actor, returned to Ealing, and died in a few days.

Mr. Henderſon performed Hamlet a ſecond time a few nights afterwards ; his feelings are deſcribed by his own words, in a letter which he wrote to a lady in London, and his reception, in ſome which he wrote to a clergyman, with whom he correſponded in the neighbourhood of London.

To

Bath, October 24th, 1772.

I AM obliged to you beyond my powers of expreſſion, for your kind ſolicitudes on my account. I haſte to anſwer them.— I had a very full houſe to the ſecond Hamlet, and I played it much better than when you ſaw me, when my terror ſunk my figure and impaired my animation.— I had a better audience ſtill laſt Tueſday to Richard, which (although I was more frightened then ever) I was much applauded for.

I am a great favorite here, if being followed at the Theatre, and invited to private

vate parties among people of confequence, are proofs of it.—I never took any thing kinder in my life than your coming to fee me; it was a mark of attention, friend-fhip, and regard, that, as I am confcious of not altogether deferving, delighted me exceedingly—It would have delighted me ftill more to have deferved it. But that you know is my fault—It fhall be cor-rected. You will find me very different in my manners.

Will you give my kind fervices to Mifs ———, though fhe is a forry jade and don't deferve them, for fhe has the info-lence to let my letter remain unanfwered. Yet, upon recollection, there may be kind-nefs in it, fhe may not be willing to engage me in a correfpondence to which I am un-equal. Adieu, my dear madam.—This is a

villainous

villainous fhort létter, but I muſt break it off,

" Leſt Benedict fhould enter full of fear."

J. COURTENAY.

To the Rev. Mr. D————

Bath, 9th October, 1772.

DEAR DOCTOR,

YOU are among thofe of my friends whom I cannot fuffer to be unaddrefs'd by this opportunity of Mr. I————'s rcturn. He will tell you my fuccefs, and you will feel that pleafure from it, which a mind and friendfhip like yours, cannot but feel, from the applaufe and approbation conferred on all you efteem and patronize.— I know, my dear fir, that I am very near

your

your heart, and I thank you, I efteem you, I love you for it. You diftinguifhed me when none elfe would; you encouraged me when others bore hard upon me. Never, never can I forget the kindnefs of your conduct towards me—Something too much of this. You muft excufe the fhortnefs of this letter, I have many to write, and very little time——Will you honour me with a line?—I cannot fay that I will anfwer it, but I will reply to it,——You will remember that my ftage name is Courtenay; to you, my dear fir, I will never fign any other than the name you gave me. I value it on that account, and therefore fubfcribe myfelf,

S H A N D Y.

To

To Mr. Henderson.

25th November, 1772.

Dear Shandy,

I cannot well defcribe the pleafure I
received from the news of your fuccefs,
without fome danger of expreffing myfelf
in terms which, by the invidious, might
perhap be conftrued into flattery. This
is one reafon why I have not anfwered
your letter before, and not preffed for-
ward among the firft lift of your congra-
tulators.

Your letter, as it feems to have been dictated by a generous heart, which accepted
the will for the deed, does you more honour than all your talents, brilliant as they
are, and would to heaven my power had

been

been equal to my inclination, to render you any effential fervices. All friends here join in the general joy at the favourable account of Mr. Courtenay's reception.

As you know my real opinion of your genius and abilities, and that I never had any doubt concerning your fuccefs, provided your voice would hold out, it would be ridiculous to take up your time in paying compliments to that merit which I hope will foon be as confpicuous to the world, as it long ago was to me.

I truft you will not think the fhort advice which I am about to give, to be altogether impertinent; although your prudence and good fenfe may render it unneceffary.

Beware then, my dear friend, of the intoxication of applaufe, and remember that

great

great application, perfeverance, caution, and continual efforts to improve, are principal, if not the only fteps which can fupport you in your afcent to the fummit of a lafting fame.

I hope you will avoid every fpecies of in-temperance, particularly that of the tongue. Do not defpife the old adage, however trite it may be: viz. " Many a man hath facri-ficed his friend for his joke."   Be the player, but be the player no where but upon the ftage.   Out of the verge of the theatre, low buffoonery from a comedian, I hold to be errant proftitution. Why fhould not he be as much the gentleman as a perfon of any other profeffion ?

I mean not to lay any reftraint, Shandy, upon the genuine fallies of innocent humour and wit, but upon that kind of pleafantry

and

and ridicule, the object of which is the degradation of character: a vein of mirth which fpecioufly pretends to exhilarate the fpirits, whilft it infidioufly wounds the heart.

Are you not ready, by this time, to break out, and to exclaim in the language of rage and impatience, " Something too much of this preaching, my dear Doctor—you do not confider that my ears are now open to no founds but the thunders of an applauding audience, and my eyes accuftomed to read nothing with pleafure, or with patience, but the *billet doux* of fome love-fick languifhing nymph."

May you, my dear Shandy, in your public performances, be always received with the heart-chearing plaudits of the ju-

dicious,

dicious, nor ever by your private conduct forfeit the efteem and approbation of the virtuous and good.

I am, &c.

To the Rev. Mr. D———.

Bath, Dec. 25, 1772.

My very Dear Doctor,

IT is fo common a thing to fill letters with excufes for their fhortnefs, and apologies for want of time, that I am almoft afhamed of doing it, and yet the true reafon I have not replied to your friendly letter, is, the intenfe fatigue of my ftudies, together with the vifits I am obliged to make; for I find it neceffary to be as attentive to my reputation out of the theatre as in it; and

don't

don't think me vain, if I fay, that the more my acquaintance is extended, the more my reputation is encreafed——Enquire of me, Doctor, I am confident you can hear no-thing of me which can difgrace your virtues to be in friendfhip with, or your genius to have diftinguifhed. I am in intimacy with a great many people of the firft rank and genius in Bath, and my connections are too polite to admit of the low buffoonery you caution me againft. I am now fituated to my heart's wifh, I converfe with men of letters, and am well received by them; I am in high favour with the manager, for which fee my letter to J. I——, a few days ago.

I have refumed my own name in a Pro-logue, written for me by a gentleman of great talents, and a painter, though not a painter by profeffion. His genius is like

the Dryades and Hamadryades, embofomed
in woods and fields.   In plain Englifh, he
is, perhaps, the greateft landfcape painter
we have :

" By heaven, and not a mafter taught."

I muft tell you fomething which I know
will pleafe you.   I am perfectly altered in
my manners.   I can now be gay and merry
without being very licentious.   I am willing to owe this to your advice, becaufe you
are among the few from whom it is not very
painful to receive obligations.

I have been on the ftage three months,
and I have played ten different characters,
all of the firft importance ; this will fhew
you how I pafs my time, and convince you that it is not poffible for me to
have many leifure hours.   Mr. Garrick has
                                               done

done me great services by writing of me to several of his friends here. I intend to write very soon to thank him for them—I thank Apollyon for his remembrance; make mine to him, and to all your family.

I am, &c.

J. HENDERSON.

To

To the Rev. Mr. D——.

DEAR DOCTOR,

I Wish to reply to your last friendly letter, but I have little or nothing to say, and scarce any time to say that little or nothing in.   It is needless to take up much time or paper, in assuring you, that I have a very great, and almost filial affection for you; for I might say that in three words, and tell you, I am grateful.

I have played Lear with very great approbation, which I know will please you, and I continue to be received with respect, and

even

even friendſhip, almoſt wherever I go. You may be aſſured I will forget none of your excellent monitions to preſerve this, and indeed I am ſo far altered that I ſeldom jeſt, and ſtill ſeldomer ridicule. I have every reaſon to be ſatisfied with having come here, for I could not have been more happy, I think, any where, and I do not doubt but that it will be for my future advantage.

The manager, I believe, eſteems me, for no man can be more diſtinguiſhed than I am by him. *.

I am extremely obliged to you for your offer as to the *Claſſicks*, and I hope to ſhew you in the ſummer, that I wiſh to improve

by

by your inſtructions. You muſt have patience, if I ſometimes diſcover too much
miſcellaneous rambling. I will be as attentive as I can.

I am, &c.

J. HENDERSON.

In the course of this season, the manager finding his new performer attracted the attention of the public, introduced him in near twenty different characters, to many of which he must have been very unequal.*

He however became popular, was spoken of by the title of the Bath Roscius, in high estimation with the frequenters of the Theatre, and distinguished by the friendship and protection of men, whose approbation will always confer honour and

G 4

create

* I have not a recollection of them all, but the principal were Hamlet, Richard the Third, Benedict, Macbeth, Bobadil, which he attempted, and very successfully performed, in the manner of Mr. Woodward; Bayes, Don Felix, Earl of Essex, Hotspur Fribble Lear, Hastings, Alonzo, and Alzuma; he accredited Garrick's Ode.

create envy,* and in confequence of this was moft unmercifully abufed in the Bath papers both for what he did, and what he did

* Lord Newnham, whofe tafte is not lefs diftinguifhed than his rank.—Mr. Gainfborough, whofe portraits exhibit, not merely the map of the countenance, but the character, the foul of the original.—His landfcapes, —But to name works which fafcinate and delight every eye, is to praife. Mr. Philip Thickneffe, whofe partiality is the more valuable, as it is neither lightly or indifcriminately beftowed. Of his warm regards, and friendly zeal, Mr. Henderfon, as well as the writer of thefe anecdotes, received many proofs. Mr. Taylor, very properly diftinguifhed, as the painter " by heaven, and not a mafter " taught;" and though laft mentioned, ever firft in kind and attentive fervices, the author of the Weft Indian.

did not do * How far their satires gave uneasiness to the object they were aimed

at,

* The following little Epigram was written, I believe, by a gentleman of Bath, who afterwards became a partial friend to Henderson, and who is a proof that good sense and candour is open to conviction, for he acknowledged that his sentence was too harsh.

EXTEMPORE,

On Mr. COURTENAY's attempting to recite Mr. Garrick's Jubilee Ode, on the 9th of Dec. 1772.

When Courtenay spouted Garrick's Ode,
How did the man mistake his road;
And void of all the rules of art,
Distracted rave through every part,
Tearing his lungs, 'till out of breath,
Wild as the witches in Macbeth,
Whilst the old Bard who stood behind,
Attentive on his arm reclin'd,

Affected

at, will appear by an extract from a letter, dated 24th May 1773.

Affected at the murther'd tale
Trembled, and as his ghost look'd pale.

   I thought the cloud-capt towers, and all
The gorgeous palaces would fall
With Shakespeare off his pedestal,
For the whole fabric tottering shook
From its foundations when he spoke;
Garrick himself, had he been by
Had died———but not in extacy.

To

To Mr. J————.

———————— There is a writer here
" who has difcovered no talent, (but judgment in his fignature) called the INVALID,
who has, I hear, abufed me and my Pro-
logue, * which has faved me a few fhil-
lings, for I was about to hire fomebody to
fatirize

* A Prologue he fpoke 22d December, 1772, upon re-
fuming his own name, which follows:

(Written by JOHN TAYLOR, Efq. of the Circus.)

WHEN firft the advent'rous bard ftands forth to
    view,
Thofe early fketches which with care he drew;
When he, poor man, in lines uncouth and lame,
Juft ventures out a candidate for fame,

Trembling

satirize me into public converſation ; the
people here having agreed to applaud me
without

Trembling, he dreads a *damned* poet's fate,
The judges ſhrug—the carping critics hate.
Some partial friend, juſt at this anxious hour,
With chearing gaiety's reviving power,
Laughs at his doubts——" Nay, prithee don't recede,
'Take courage man !—My word for't you'll ſucceed ;
Out with your works, and let the world decide
On their true merit—while your name you hide."
This fancy ſtrikes his weak diſtracted brain,
He ſmiles, and ſimpering, ſays, he'll write again.
Aye——but have patience, Tom, his friend replies ;
The world—the world, my lad, has piercing eyes ;
Mankind firſt try—by them alone be chear'd,
Their praiſe be courted, or their cenſure fear'd.
——The piece comes out by Tom, John, Dick, or
    Harry,
No matter which—perhaps it may miſcarry.
But no—the learn'd approve and praiſe the ſtyle,
The ladies read it—e'en the critics ſmile.

without much enquiry why or wherefore.

Mr.

Straight to his friend he runs, to tell the news.
The world, dear fir, my work with pleafure views;
The firft edition, fir, I juft now hear,
Is quite run off——a fecond will appear,
And fince that met the applaufe I wifh'd to feel,
May I not now my real name reveal?

Ye candid fair, while wav'ring here I ftand,
In fad fufpence—O lend a helping hand;
May I, protected by your foftering care,
When critics murmur, to your court repair;
I have, alas! on this wide fea of fame,
Launch'd my poor bark, under a feigned name,
That if your frowns foretold a boifterous gale,
I might in time have lower'd my fhiv'ring fail; *
Have foon retreated from the ftormy main,
And hopelefs fhrunk into my port again.

May

* Shivering, a fea term when a fail is not wholly filled with the wind,
nor quite aback, as the feamen fay.

Mr. Colman has done me some service
of that sort, for which I always bow very
low to him, and he takes it for respect.*

The

May your kind favour still to me be shewn;
My merit pleads not—make the act your own;
And since you've deign'd to approve my weak essays,
From princely Hamlet, down to puzzling Bayes,
I now, with trembling hand the mask resign,
And hence appear before this beauteous shrine.
————————Courtenay no more!
O name so flattering to my fame-sick heart,
I bid farewell—we now, though friends, must part.
To thee thy borrower grateful tribute pays,
With thee, he hopes, not now to lose your praise.
Shine still propitious!—Still your smiles renew,
And Courtenay's pains in Henderson review;
Perfect the work that's now but rudely form'd,
And save the fruit, which in the bud you warm'd.

* Mr. Colman said, when Henderson performed
Shylock, his dress was so shabby it seemed just borrowed
from

'The tide of partiality being high in his favour, he had in contemplation the purchafe of a fourth fhare in the Briftol Theatre. The money was provided, when he declined embarking in the fcheme, for reafons which appear in the following letter.

To

from a pawn-broker, and gave him the idea of a black Lear."

This cenfure falls with more weight upon the manager of the wardrobe, than the performer, and bears more refemblance to the cavil of a French taylor, than the candid critique one would have expected from the author of the Jealous Wife.

To Mr. I———:

Sunday Night, Nov. 1, 1772.

DEAR FRIEND,

THIS is the information I have gathered. The moft money that has been
paid for any fhare has been four hundred
pounds. There are four partners at 400l.
each, and one of them (the not acting manager) has forty pounds a feafon allowed
him for his intereft of the 400l. together
with the freedom of the Theatre for himfelf,
family, and friends. Three hundred pounds
a feafon is paid for the rent, and the fifty
proprietors are admitted gratis to all performances whatfoever at the Theatre, which
is thought much overloaded. It was rather
a lofing fcheme to Powell and Holland. It

is

is known that Mr. King loſt above eighty pounds the ſeaſon he held it; and the laſt ſeaſon, 'tis ſaid, each partner loſt between one and two hundred pounds.

The whole property belonging to the partners, of clothes, ſcenes, &c. is ſuppoſed to be worth under a thouſand pounds, and there are only two years to come of the leaſe. There are three votes of the three acting managers in the conduct of the theatre.

There is no patent, which ſubjects the managers to this inconvenience, that as their performers are not engaged by forms of law, they can quit them when they pleaſe.

Theſe are the informations I have collected. It really does not ſtrike me as any thing ſo devoutly to be wiſhed for. I can never ceaſe to love you, my dear friend, for

the

the extreme folicitude you exprefs on this account. I really feel your zeal to ferve me, will, from its precipitance, go too far. I am myfelf utterly unqualified to manage players, and I muft be at the difcretion of * * * * * * * * * * * *,

Do, pray Jack, weigh it well. I have thefe informations from an authority you could not doubt, if I were at liberty to mention it—I am perfuaded, that if I chufe to play in the fummer at Briftol, I may make almoft my own terms, and then I have nothing to lofe,

It will be a great charge upon my mind, and I have need of all the time, attention and ftudy, I can have, to preferve the reputation I have got here. Another thing is, I fhall want fome recefs from the fatigues of the feafon, and my chief hope and

ambition

ambition is, to pafs the fummer with you, and my other friends.

There may be foon a time when your kindnefs may find a more ferviceable exercife, and I am affured from your extreme goodnefs in this, that it will not lofe any of its ardour. You will obferve, that four hundred pounds is the moft that ever was given for any fhare, *and be afks* 400l.

I am of a patient, philofophical temper, and can live as well upon the little pittance I have as if it was larger, at leaft 'till my acquaintance is fuch as will require an additional expence in clothes.

In three words, I have not fet my heart upon it; on the contrary, if it is fecured for me, I fhall enter upon it with trepidation and doubt. I know L—— grounds

his

his opinion of its fuccefs, upon the favourable reception I have met with here. But the people of Briftol, I fuppofe, are like other people, capricious, inconftant.

The theatre was fupported, it feems, by them for one feafon, but after that it flagged even when *Powell* was there.

Adieu, the bell rings.

J. COURTENAY.

When the Bath theatre clofed, he returned to London, and in his hours of unguarded pleafantry, frequently gratified himfelf and friends by ludicrous imitations of the different performers, particularly Mr. Garrick, who being informed that Henderfon's voice was fuch an echo of the greenroom, invited him to a breakfaft, and requefted a fpecimen of his art. The three firft examples were Barry, Woodward, and Love, and happy would it have been for Henderfon had he concluded there. Mr. Garrick appeared in extacy at the imitation; but, Sir, faid he, you'll kill poor Barry, flay Woodward, and break Love's heart! Your ear muft be wonderfully correct, and your voice moft fingularly flexible—I am told you *have me.* Do, my dear Sir, let me hear what I am, for if you are equally exact with me as with Barry and Woodward, I fhall know precifely what my peculiar tones

are——

are—*Henderson* excused himself, by saying, that Mr. Garrick's powers were superior to imitation, that he would not presume to attempt it, and begged leave to decline so hazardous an undertaking, in which he was conscious any man *must* fail ; but the other two gentlemen pressing him to comply, he, " *in evil hour confented,*" and gave imitations from Benedict. The voice was so exact as to delight the two auditors—But for Mr. Garrick ; he sat in sullen silence for half a minute, then walked across the room with an exclamation, " that egad, if, if, if that was his voice, he had never known it himself ; for, upon his foul, it was entirely dissimilar to every thing he conceived *his* to be, and totally unlike any found that had ever struck upon his ear until that moment." So very unfair judges are we of whatever touches our own vanity, and so fore at whatever wounds our own pride.

The

The great hero of the drama, the man upon whom, if we may believe Paul White-head, the taſte and virtue of a poliſhed nation depended,* could not bear to contemplate his own figure in the mirror which he often held up, and where he was delighted to view others.

Tremblingly alive, he ſhuddered at the ſhadow of ridicule; and felt as much from the apprehenſion of a paultry epigram by an obſcure news-paper ſcribbler, as Foote would have done from a volume of ſatire againſt himſelf, with the name of Churchill in the title page.

Who would wiſh to poſſeſs ſuch exceſs of irritability ? He ſeriouſly complained Mr.

 Henderſon

* " A nation's taſte depends on you,

" Perhaps a nation's virtue too."

Henderſon went about the town taking him off, and that he poſted him in every company.

A conſciouſneſs of his own well-earned celebrity might have furniſhed him with ſufficient armour againſt ſuch attacks, and upon many other occaſions he ſeemed to poſſeſs this conſciouſneſs in a very high degree.

Previous to this time, Mr. Pingo, by direction of Mr. Garrick, engraved a medal, on one ſide of which was the manager's head. On the reverſe three figures, that reſembled plague, peſtilence, and famine, more than what they were intended to repreſent, namely *the three Graces*, with this modeſt inſcription,

" He has united all your powers."

This being by a gentleman to whom Mr. Garrick had prefented it, fhewn to Hender-fon, when at my table with a number of his friends, he repeated the following little impromptu, which I think deferves the name of a good epigram.

Three fqualid hags, when Pingo form'd,
  And chriften'd them the *graces*;
Garrick, with Shakefpeare's magic warm'd,
  Recogniz'd foon their faces.

He knew them for the fifters weird,
  Whofe art bedimm'd the noon-tide hour,
And from his lips this line was heard,
  " *I have united all your power.*"

So Garrick, critics all agree,
  The graces help'd thee to no riches,
And Pingo thus to flatter thee,
  Has made *his* graces witches.

So long was this great man accuftomed
to adulation, it became at laft neceffary to
his dramatic exiftence, and fo eager was
he to intercept the fhafts that were aimed
againft him, that he held up to obfervation what would, without his interpofition,
have fallen to the ground, and funk un-
marked into oblivion.   This might have
been the fate of the imitations, but Mr.
Garrick gave fome confequence to them,
and the fpeaker, by his notice.*

Mr. Henderfon's friends had different
opinions refpecting the propriety of making

---

* I think it was Boerhaave, who being afked, why
he did not write anfwers to fome pamphlets which were
written againft his medical fyftem, replied, he thought
of them as fparks upon the pages of his books, which he
only had the power of blowing into a flame, but let alone
they would go out of themfelves.

ing Mr. Garrick his model. I have inferted two letters, in which that circumftance is mentioned, written by a gentleman
who honoured him with his friendſhip
and protection, the firſt feaſon he played
at Bath.

To

Bath, 27th June, 1773.

DEAR HENDERSON,

IF you had not wrote to me as you did, I should have concluded you had been laid down ; pray, my boy, take care of yourself this hot weather, and don't run about London streets, fancying you are catching strokes of *nature,* at the hazard of your constitution——It was my first school, and deeply read in petticoats I am, therefore you may allow me to caution you.

Stick to Garrick as close as you can for your life : you should follow his heels like his shadow in sunshine.

No

No one can be so near him as yourself when you please, and I'm sure when he sees it strongly as other people do, he must be fond of such an *ape*. You have nothing to do now but to stick to the few great ones of the earth, who seem to have offered you their assistance in bringing you to light, and to brush off all the low ones as fast as they light upon you. —You see I hazard the appearing a puppy in your eyes, by pretending to advise you, from the real regard, and sincere desire I have of seeing you a great and happy man. —Garrick is the greatest creature living in every respect, he is worth studying in every action.—Every view and every idea of him is worthy of being stored up for imitation, and I have ever found him a generous and sincere friend. Look upon him, Henderson, with your imitative eyes, for when he drops you'll have nothing but

poor

poor old nature's book to look in.—You'll
be left to grope it out alone, ſcratching your
pate in the dark, or by a farthing candle.
— .. Now is your time, my lively fellow
——And do ye hear, don't eat ſo devi-
liſhly ; you'll get too fat when you reſt
from playing, or get a ſudden jogg by
illneſs to bring you down again. *   *
*   *   *   *   *   *   *

Adieu, my dear H,

believe me your's, &c.

T. G.

To Mr. HENDERSON.

Bath, July 18, 1773.

DEAR HENDERSON,

I F one may judge by your laſt ſpirited epiſtle you are in good keeping, no one eats with a more grateful countenance, or ſwallows with more good nature than yourſelf.

If this does not ſeem ſenſe, do but re-collect how many hard featured fellows there are in the world that frown in the midſt of enjoyment, chew with unthank-fulneſs, and ſeem to ſwallow with pain inſtead of pleaſure ; now any one who ſees you eat pig and plumb ſauce, imme-diately *feels that pleaſure* which a plump morſel,

morſel, ſmoothly gliding through a narrow glib paſſage into the regions of bliſs, and moiſtened with the dews of imagination, naturally creates.

Some iron-faced dogs you know ſeem to chew dry ingratitude, and ſwallow diſcontent. Let ſuch be kept to *under parts,* and never truſted to ſupport a character. —In all but eating ſtick to Garrick ;— In *that* let him ſtick to you, for I'll be curſt if you are not his maſter.— Never mind the fools who talk of imitation and copying—All is imitation, and if you quit that natural likeneſs to Garrick which your mother beſtowed upon you, you'll be flung ——Aſk Garrick elſe.

Why, ſir, what makes the difference between man and man, is real performance,

and

and not genius or conception.—There are a thoufand Garrick's, a thoufand Giardini's, and Fifher's, and Abels. Why only one Garrick, with Garrick's eyes, voice, &c. &c. &c? One Giardini with Giardini's fingers, &c. &c. But one Fifher with Fifher's dexterity, quicknefs, &c? Or more than one Abel with Abel's feeling upon the inftrument? All the reft of the world are mere *bearers* and *fee'ers.*

Now, as I faid in my laft, as nature feems to have intended the fame thing in you as in Garrick, no matter how fhort or how long, her kind intention muft not be croffed.——If it is, fhe will tip the wink to madam fortune, and you'll be kicked down ftairs.————

" Think on that Mafter Ford."

God blefs you,

I   T. G.

Mr. Garrick, however, as well as the other managers, frequently heard him rehearfe both at his own houfe and upon the ftage, treated him with polite attention, and acted with apparent kindnefs and good nature.

At one of thefe rehearfals was prefent Mr. George Garrick, who, being afked if he would ftay and hear Mr. Henderfon, faid he would do himfelf that pleafure, *merely as a fpectator.* But he found a very fpeedy occafion of objection, and faid that in one inftance it appeared to him the fpeaker miftook the character. "Egad, my dear Brother," faid Mr. Garrick, "you moft egregioufly miftake your own character; you told us juft now you would remain a *Spectator,* you forget what you are, and turn *Tatler;* but never mind, George,

George, Mr. Henderſon, whatever he is, depend upon me being the *Guardian*."

Some of the other managers deigned to think him *well enough* for Bath, but totally unfit for the boards of a London Theatre, and one of the players obſerved, that, " Though he appeared a meteor in the Bath *horizon*, he would be but a farthing candle in the London *hemiſphere*." The gentleman's meaning I am not bound to explain, for it is not neceſſary for the collector of a few ſcattered anecdotes to be a philoſopher, but I dare ſay many of his friends recollect the remark, for it was made in the green-room.

Flattered by ſuch encomiums, and gratified by ſuch teſtimonies of approbation from his brethren of the buſkin, on the

 24th

24th of September 1774, Mr. John Henderson returned to Bath, to gather his second crop of Somerſetſhire laurels.

During this ſeaſon he encreaſed his connections, ſtrengthened his reputation, and to the characters he had already performed, added thoſe of Zanga, Pierre, Don John, Sir John Brute, Bellville in the School for Wives, Henry the Second, Beverly in the Man of Buſineſs, Archer, Ranger, Comus, and Othello.

In the part of Othello I never ſaw him, but, by his own account, it was not ſuccefsful; and ſhall we wonder at his failure in that which eluded the graſp of Mr. Garrick. It was too mighty for him.

To Barry, the wonder working-Barry, and to him only, ſeemed to be given the

full

full powers for exhibiting the markings of this moſt difficult part.

" But Barry's magic cannot copied be."

Amongſt the multitudes of candidates who have choſen to make their firſt appearance in this character, attracted, I believe, by its having, like Richard the Third, a ſonorous ſound, and giving them a power of maſking their terrors under a black face, how few have tolerably ſucceeded.

The Moor, is conceived with all the tremendous dignity of Shakeſpeare, and demands a portion of that fire which illumined the mighty maſter of the drama, to give him body and colouring to an audience.

I 3

Mr.

Mr. Henderson informed me, that on his first appearance in Othello, the manager had habited him in so ridiculous a garb, that he wanted nothing but the brush and scraper, to give a compleat resemblance of a chimney sweeper on May-day, and that he was certain it exceeded all power of face, to avoid smiling at least at so ludicrous a figure.

This disconcerted him so much, as to check his effusions, of which circumstance, he never so totally lost the recollection, as to appear in this character without some embarrasment.

That his want of success was not owing to his want of application, will appear by the following letter to the Bath manager;

nager; which should induce us to make
every allowance for the errors of the
performer in a new character, which he
is frequently obliged to personate, without time for the proper and neceffary
confideration,

To

To Mr. PALMER, at Bath.]

London, August 3, 1773.

DEAR SIR,

I Have received Othello and your letters, to which I do not tell you that I will pay attention, but that *I am* attending to both. But it will be utterly impoffible that I fhould come down prepared for acting thofe parts you mention immediately. I never did, nor ever fhall repine, at the quantity, or the variety of bufinefs you employ me in, but furely it muft be for your intereft as well as my credit, to have me ftudied in the parts I am to appear in, and not to let me go on the ftage in the hafty, crude, and unprepared manner I have done. Mr. Garrick fays, " he has heard that I fwallowed my

parts

parts like an eager glutton, and ſpewed my undigeſted fragments in the face of the audience." The figure is nauſeous, but not more nauſeous than juſt.

You may be aſſured, my dear Sir, that I have no powers, or faculties of any ſort, which I would not exert in your ſervice. I may be deficient, but indolent I will never be. I muſt obſerve to you, that a thouſand incorrectneſſes, haſtineſſes, and errors, which the people excuſed in my firſt appearance, will not be ſo indulgently confidered the ſecond ſeaſon, and for that reaſon I hope you will not expect I ſhould run through ſuch a haſty ſucceſſion of characters; and I hope too that you will confider this obſervation not as an idle apology for lazineſs, but a ſerious appeal to your judgment and your friendſhip. It is ten to one but you laugh at this, but let me aſſure you, upon the

credit

credit of experience, that to keep ten or fifteen characters, of great magnitude, importance and variety, diftinct and ftrong upon the mind and memory, is no trifling bufinefs. To learn words, indeed, is no great labour, and to pour them out no very difficult matter. It is done on our ftage almoft every night; but with what fuccefs, I leave you to judge. The generality of performers think it enough to learn the words, and thence all that vile uniformity and unvaried manner which difgraces the theatre.

I faw Mr. Garrick yefterday, and he has promifed to go over fome fcenes with me on Monday next.

As for *Othello*, I tremble at it: 'tis a mighty and an arduous tafk; but I begin to take great pleafure in it, and will bend it

to

to my powers, if I cannot raise them to it. But for God's sake, my dear friend, let me have time to weigh it well. Mr. Garrick assures me, he was upwards of two months rehearsing Benedict, before he could satisfy himself that he had modelled his action and recital to his own idea of the part.

You will hurt me very much, if you think I have any vain or idle motives for what I say. I do really feel that one strong and powerful idea in the mind for a while overwhelms and extrudes all others, and he who hopes to succeed in Othello, or any part of such dignity and moment, must give all his powers of thought and fancy to that, and that alone, till it is impressed upon the memory strong enough to remain unshaken by the streams of lighter images which pass it. You will laugh, as we both did, at somebody else, if I intimate, it is for the honour

of

of your theatre that I wish to tread it with the marks of thinking, and attention, and study on me, and therefore I am content to solicit, as an indulgence to myself, that I may be allowed time to deliberate on my future characters. This I will venture to say, you will not repent agreeing to my request, for in the mind I am now in, I see so clearly the value of the reputation I hazard, that nothing can or shall divert me from the most sedulous application. As I write to the friend as well as the manager, I will add, that my industry shall have your advantage for part of its motive. I very sincerely hope Mrs. Palmer will recover her health, and you your happiness. I have a most perfect value and affection for you both, which, whether you either of you believe or not, I will ever preserve, and so God bless you.

Gainsborough

Gainſborough is a varlet, he promiſed me a miniature from the picture of mine, but wits and genius', if they get nothing elſe from the court, learn their d——d tricks of promiſing and forgetting. * * * * * *

* * * * * * * * * * * * * *

You are miſtaken in me. I fence almoſt every day, and ſtudy much, and eat little. I mean compared to your character of me. I think you had better write to Mr. Garrick about that lady. I have not ſeen Mrs. Greville, but have heard great things of her at Mr. G——s (the author), and from ſeveral others. I intend to go to Richmond this week.

J. H.

At

At the expiration of this second Bath feafon, with united teftimonies of approbation from many who were deemed good judges of theatric merit, he returned to London, where he paffed the few months of his recefs. During this period, he frequently rehearfed, and read to Mr. Garrick, Mr. Foote*, Mr. Harris, and Mr. Leake,

but

* At fome of thefe rehearfals I was prefent, but Mr. Thomas Davies has given a defcription of one of them, in which he exhibits fo true a picture of that moft eccentric character, the late Sam Foote, that I hope I fhall be pardoned for inferting it.

* Before Henderfon left London, he was advifed to try if Mr. Foote would not give him an opportunity of fhewing bimfelf at his theatre in the Haymarket. Two friends accompanied him to North End. Our modern Ariftophanes welcomed the vifitants with great civility ; but fuch is the volatility of his genius, that it was not poffible to announce the errand immediately : he muft be

permitted

but his fate was to find all of them,
" Damn with faint praife."

It

permitted to indulge his peculiar humour, and to let off
a few voluntaries, before he could be induced to hear of
any bufinefs whatfoever. Foote's imagination is fo
lively, and his conceptions fo rapid, as well as exuberant,
that his converfation is a cataract, or torrent of wit, humour, pleafantry, and fatire. The company had fcarce
unfolded their bufinefs, when he gave them the hiftory
of Sir Gregory Grinwell and Lady Barbary Bramble.
The whimfical fituations into which he put his characters
with his lively and farcaftic remarks, threw the company into convulfions of laughter.

" However, Henderfon's friends thought it was now
time to ftop the current of Mr. Foote's vivacities, by
informing him of the reafon of their vifit. One of
them took the lead :—

" Sir, our young friend, the Bath Rofcius, would
think himfelf extremely happy to have the opinion of fo
acknowledged a judge of theatrical merit as you are ;
he

It was, however, the earnest wish of his friends, that he should appear upon the

London

he wishes you would permit him to rehearse a scene of a play."

" Well, Sir, what are you for, the sock or the buskin? I'll be hanged if you are not quite enamoured of that bouncing brimstone Tragedy."—"Mr. Henderson is not confined, Sir, to either."—" Stick to the sock, young gentleman; the one is all nature, and the other all art and trick. Tragedy is mere theatrical bombast, the very fungus of the theatre. Come, Sir, give us a taste of your quality."—Here Henderson began a speech in Hamlet; when Foote, turning round to one of the company, said, " Have you not heard in what manner this impudent little scoundrel has treated me ?"—" I protest, Sir, I don't know whom you mean."—" No, where have you left your apprehension? Let me but tell you what a damned trick he served me lately, by lending me a large sum of money."—" Consider, my dear Sir, the time grows late, and we are to dine in town."—" No, no," said Foote, " you shall dine with me upon

a stewed

London ſtage, and try if the public would
be more indulgent than the directors of their
amuſements;

a ſtewed rump of beef, and a diſh of fiſh." Now Mr.
Henderſon begins. Well, once more he endeavoured
to open, when behold, an unlucky joke, *a petite hiſloirs,*
ſome droll thought, or ſome unaccountable idea, prevented the diſconcerted actor from diſplaying his powers
of elocution: his caſe was now become extremely
pitiable.

However, after hearing this ſingular genius read an
act of his new comedy, take off Lady Betty Biggamy,
recite the whole trial of himſelf and George Faulkener,
ridicule the Iriſh Lord Chief Juſtice Robinſon, for con-
demning his Peter Paragraph for a libel, ſpeak a Pro-
logue in the character of Peter, laugh at our moſt celebrated orators of the bar, mimic the members of both
Houſes of Parliament, tell ſome ludicrous ſtories of Cap-
tain Bodens and the Iriſh chairman, Henderſon was
permitted to repeat, without interruption, Mr. Garrick's
Prologue, which he ſpoke on his firſt appearance, after
his arrival from the Continent. This being no cari-

caturc,

amusements; but this step he himself was not very earnest to take, unless he could be received upon terms, which it was not very easy to procure. By *terms*, I do not mean salary; that was not the principal object,

but

cature, but a genuine and fair representation of the great Roscius's manner, without the least exaggeration, we cannot be surprised that it did not make any impression upon Mr. Foote; however, he paid the speaker a compliment upon the goodness of his ear. Dinner was now announced; every thing was princely, and in splendid order. Wit flew about the table: I mean Mr. Foote's; for I would advise every man that has any wit of his own, who shall have the honour to dine with this gentleman, to bottle it up for another occasion; for he is himself master of enough, and to spare, for ten companies. I need not observe that many portraits were drawn, and some of them in a masterly stile.

When Henderson took his leave of him, he whispered one of the company in the ear, *" that he would not do."* Mr. Foote confirmed the death-warrant that had been already signed by *Garrick, Colman, Harris,* and *Leake.*

but exemption from being forced upon characters for which he was unqualified, in
which his confequent failure would have
blighted his budding honours, and funk
him into the obfcurity he fo much dreaded.
Somewhat chagrined at the reception which
had been given him by the monarchs of the
theatre, in September, 1774, he returned
to Bath.

That his mortification had not wholly
fubdued his pleafantry, appears from the
following letter, which he wrote a few days
previous to his leaving London, to a friend
who was then at Margate.

To

To Mr. I————.

London, Sept. 21, 1774.

A S there is an expreſs coming to thee, I ſhall write, otherwiſe it would not have been worth thy while to have paid a groat for what thou haſt ſo often paid for before, and that is my lov.. I hope thou art become an inhabitant of the deep waters by this time, and wilt give me an account of the vegetation of coral, and the venereal amuſements of ſharks and lampreys;—ſay nothing to the women, but tell me privately, whether the porpoiſe hath that amorous alacrity which the fat ones of the earth ſo much wonder at, and whether there be any ſuch thing as conjugal fidelity among the herrings and the lobſters of the ocean. As for the reſt, thanks for the draft, which I ſhall not uſe,

becauſe

because foreseeing that the waves would cling longer about your waist than you at first imagined, I applied to your friend H.

Adieu,

J. HENDERSON.

P. S. I set out from your house for Bath on Sunday morning. My week's business is as follows: Monday, Hamlet; Tuesday, Benedict; Wednesday, Belville.

His

His reception at Bath was in the higheft degree gratifying. Men, to whofe decifions the world paid implicit obedience, diftinguifhed his talents, invited him to their tables, and admitted him as the companion of their feftive hours, where his eafy humour and lively pleafantry enfured him a moft welcome reception. But this pleafantry was not fufficiently guarded. In the hours of merriment and laughter, he was often afked for imitations, and Mr. Garrick being the *Magnus Apollo* of the drama, whofe actions were obvious to all, and of whofe manners no one was ignorant, Mr. Henderfon was frequently requefted to exhibit him. The inconveniences he had formerly felt had not taught him caution; he continued the fame practice, and with more accuracy than prudence, gave the little ftories of the day, and entered fo forcibly into the manner of that great man, that

every

every hearer was ftruck with the refemblance. This was a freedom Mr. Garrick
could not forgive. For a young theatrical
adventurer, upon a country ftage, and confequently dependant upon him for an introduction to Drury-lane, to make *his* peculiarities the object of imitation, was a fin
never to be forgiven, and perhaps one fource
of the difficulties he found, in his attempts
af an introduction to a London theatre,

At Bath he, however, encreafed his dramatic reputation, and performed in either
play or farce, four or five times a week.
He added to his lift of characters, amongft
many others, thofe of Ford, Pofthumus,
Shylock, Lorenzo in the Spanifh Friar,
Sciolto, and Morcar in Matilda.

Many of his friends thought he was
wafting that time at Bath which might be
K 4

employed

employed with more advantage to his purfe, and without hazard to his reputation, in London; but he himfelf reafoned fomewhat differently, and, in this inftance, evïnced, that a cautious prudence, a quick eye to what conftituted his own intereft, and a perfevering judgment to purfue it, were ftrong *traits* in his character.

The newfpapers of the day gave a very ferious recital of this bufinefs, with all the dignity of hiftory, and all the air of authority; but as thefe grave writers were not perfectly mafters of *data* on which to ground their arguments, they have cenfured him for errors of which he was not guilty, and defended motives by which he was not actuated.

His

His own reasonings may, I should apprehend, best appear from his own letters, written to different friends, with whom he then lived in habits of the most unreserved confidence.

To Mr. I———,

Bath, October 24th, 1774.

MY MOST DEAR FRIEND,

DON'T think me careless of your advice, or of my own affairs, becaufe I did not write to you by return of the poft. The importance of the matter, made ftill more important by your inter-ference, refolved me to think moft deliber-ately and attentively on it, before I formed my conclufions.—I have now, I think, confidered it amply, and compared the advantages with the hazards—you will be convinced, that no *money interefts* have influence on my decifions, when I tell you, that I have refolved to ftay here fome time longer.—" What has then ?" you will afk.

—Repútation.

—Reputation.—" Reputation, fay you, my good friend, why that will be loft in Bath, and London will eftablifh it." I think not fo, and I will tell you why. Nothwithftanding I have played forty parts here, there are not more than five or fix which I dare offer to a London audience, on account of the fame I *have* acquired.—So fmall a number will not carry me through a feafon, and if they would, I could not have them to myfelf, becaufe I fhould not be allowed to keep even thofe parts, as it is a rule in London, not to difpoffefs any performer of thofe characters which he is thought in any degree to deferve to fup-port.—I muft then be forced upon others in which I have no merit, or none that will fupport the name I have got, and you would have the mortification to fee your friend finking into infignificance, and liv-ing a kind of rent-charge upon the The-atre.

atre. No advantage of *benefit* whatever would compensate *that*. The reasons I give for staying here, are, I think, powerful ones. I am not ripe enough for London, and what a fool of a gardener would he be who should send a basket of *green* peaches to market, when, if he had stayed a little while longer, he might have sent them ripened and rich flavoured. "*A foolish figure, but farewell it, for I will use no art.*"——You Jack, and myself, and all my friends, have mistaken my talents—we used to think that their liveliness and vigour would force them into reputation, but I find now that they require the most sedulous correction—In short, I must study, and I will make this place my college, 'till I have brought my talents to be much more like perfection than they are at present, that you and the rest

of

of my friends need not blush at the encomiums you have either silently, or openly, bestowed upon me. If you was to see me play Hamlet now, you would scarce know it to be the same person you saw before, and those who *do* see it *now*, will, I hope, soon be convinced that they shall see it still better. It is a real truth, that I feel my mind enlarges, and my powers invigorate very sensibly—you'll say, would they not do the same in London?——I answer, *no*. The continual practice I am in here is of great advantage to me—I once thought it an hardship to be forced upon so many characters, I think so now no longer, being convinced that almost every part I play, however unsuited to my nature, and however ill I may appear in it, does me good; in London it would do me harm; for this reason : there are com-

puted

puted to be *thirty* different audiences in London, here there are but *two* at the utmoſt, and thoſe of them who ſee me to a diſadvantage one night, ſee me to advantage the *next*.—I appeal to the world whether I am loſing myſelf here.

As to ſalary, that will be raiſed, and Palmer has told me, that a bank-note of fifty pounds is ready for me, when I pleaſe, for my ſervices laſt year. I will ſoon convince you, my kindeſt friend, that I want no money—It is true that I have not any, but conſider, I am a ſtudent—when I have gone through my claſſes, and can give a good tranſlation of Shakeſpeare to the world I will publiſh it, and I will preſent you with a copy, bound and gilt, if not lettered, in as good a calves-ſkin as I can procure.

Adieu,

Adieu———I will reply to the other parts of your letter when I have more leisure.

J. HENDERSON.

To Mrs. I————

Bath, 22d December, 1774.

I AM sure by your letter that it was written in the very spirit of friendship, and I have not been more gratified a great while than in reading it. I thank you most earnestly for your concern and attention to my interests: to shew you what confidence I have in your sincerity and *secresy*, (though the foolish world will not allow that virtue to your sex) I will explain to you more private and personal reasons for my not being eager to come to London, than I have written to E————, or to my dearest J————. They are not for the world to know, and E———— and Jack may shew

my

my letters to them, to all the world, *by my
choice.*

You are to know then that I think
Mr. Garrick has acted very *illiberally* and
ungentlemanly in my regard.——I will tell
you *how.* Mr. C———d sent to me the
other morning, after my playing Benedict,
to compliment and applaud me. He
told me that he was astonished at my
performance, that Mr. Garrick had prepared him for a very different opinion.——
Mr. C———d then shewed me a letter
from him, wherein he says, " See Henderson more than once, and give me your
real opinion of him."——Mr. C———d
did so, and that opinion was the most
kind and favourable that could be imagined.
Yet Mr. G——— took no manner of
notice of it, though he constantly wrote
to Mr. C———d. Mr. Garrick then

L

tampers

tampers with E————, whom you know the honour of being thought of Mr. Garrick's counsel would incline to any thing. *He* immediately tells Jack and my friends what a favourable opportunity there is for me, and they, eager to serve me, think I should jump at it. Mr. Garrick, then, to use a scripture phrase, " *Ploughs with my heifer.*"————Now the scheme appears to me thus in Mr. G————'s plan.———— Let Henderson be tempted by his friends, and by his own ambition, to come to London, he will then *apply to me*, and I can make my own conditions, he will then be considered as one whom I patronize, and protect; whereas if I apply to *him*, he will make conditions with *me*, and from my acknowledging the *want* of him, I cannot have him at my *beck.*

I did

I did not however swallow the bait so greedily as was imagined; and the confequence is that Mr. George Garrick has applied to me, but for the reafons I have written my dear I———, I declined his offer. When I talk of conditions, I defire to be underftood, my friend, that I do not mean *pecuniary* ones, if they had been my object I fhould not ftay *here*. To give you ftill farther proof that they are not, Mr. C———d told me the other night, that he was afhamed of the part Mr. Garrick had acted in this affair, and that he would undertake to get me whatever terms I pleafed at Covent-Garden, which, he added, was the houfe I muft think of whenever I came to London. * * *

* * * * * * * * * * * * * *

* * * * * * * * * * * * *. He wifhes too, he fays, that I would not make my engagement for fo long as *three*

years,

years, but I ought not to regard that, becaufe *if I make myfelf of real importance,* the forfeiture of my articles will be no impediment to my leaving Bath, and if I do not make myfelf of real importance, neither you nor any real friend will wifh to fee me there.

As to pofting Mr. Garrick, I have explained the whole affair to George Garrick, who was fatisfied, and Palmer wrote to Mr. G. to take the whole fault upon himfelf, if there was any fault. So that Mr. Garrick cannot be difpleafed with me. * * * * * * * * * *. ———I hope a little time will convince you that I am right.

Mr. C———d behaves to me with remarkable complaifance and refpect, and laft night, after my playing Shylock, he

came

came to me, and said that he was sorry he could not stay here long enough to interest himself at my benefit, that he should regret leaving Bath without giving some instance of the respect he had for my genius, and return for the pleasure it had given him, he therefore offered me a new Tragedy for my benefit, if I thought it would advantage me.

Since this is a letter of private sentiments, you must allow me to indulge a little vanity, and please myself with telling you, that Lord N———m, a nobleman who commands the taste of a numerous party of literati, and of wits, &c. came behind the scenes to me last night, with two other gentlemen, to thank me for my Shylock, and his lordship was pleased to say, it was the most finished piece of acting he ever saw, and that it far exceeded Macklin's.

In

In one word——if I thought I should never be a better actor than I am, I would not hesitate to be in London, but I will endeavour to make myself respectable and important before I come.

I hope, my very dear friend, that you see my conduct and my reasoning in a right point of view, and I flatter myself there is some resolution and firmness in my mind, since I can resist so alluring a temptation, and

" Stick to poverty with peace of mind."

Declamations, are often and reasonably suspected of having no other motive than the glitter of period, or the loftiness of language, but I *act*, as well as argue.

God

God blefs you, my good girl, I have written to an immeafureable length, but I would have you poffeffed of my rea-fons for the feeming negligence of my conduct in this affair.

J. HENDERSON.

To

To Mr. I———.

Bath, Dec. 26, 1774.

SOMEHOW or other, my dear Jack, neither you nor Mrs. I—— fee this affair right. In the firft place, Garrick did not defire E——s to bid me make my own propofal, or if he did, E——s did not explain that to me. Thefe are his words—" I faw Mr. Garrick this afternoon; we talked of you. He afked me, if you wifhed to play the enfuing winter at Drury-lane, and if fo, why you did not write to him; that if you two could agree, *" he was ready to engage you."*

In the next place, ye are wrong in fuppofing that Mr. George Garrick *called on me; he did not.* I met him in the ftreet,

and

and that morning a paragraph had appeared in the Bath papers concerning my having refolved to renew my engagements here. Mr. George Garrick's words to me, after the firft falutations, were, as nearly as I can recollect: " I had a letter from my brother, defiring me to call upon you, and hear if you had any thing to propofe for the next winter, but as I fee by the papers you have engaged again here, *it is very well.*" I replied, that I had not figned articles, but that I had almoft promifed Mr. Palmer to ftay with him, becaufe I thought this a very proper *fchool* for me—I then explained to him the nature of the miftake about *pofting* his brother, and we parted.

I wonder you can think *I bear myfelf too high*, when I confent to ftay here a poor provincial, when I might be at a

theatre

theatre in London. I can quote as well as you :

———" *Thou keep'st me from the light.*"

Again,

" *I'm sharing spoil before the field is won;*
" *Clarence still breathes, Edward still lives and reigns,*
" *When they are gone, then must I count my gains.*"

I have this morning had conversation with Mr. Cumberland ; he advises me to engage here, but only to engage from year to year—he promises to procure me an engagement at either theatre, equal to that of *Smith,* or *Reddish,* or *Lee.* The only dread I have, is, that of being put upon inferior characters—'till Garrick leaves the stage, I *must* at his theatre. There is more in the possession of characters than you seem to think. Mr. G. Garrick himself told Mr. C——d, that I should have *two trial parts,* but they

afterwards

afterwards muſt devolve to their preſent poſ-
ſeſſors. Do only, my beloved friend, think
what I muſt do *then*.

You know, whilſt you urge the *town* as
a reaſon to me, that the town do not inter-
fere. How was *Lee*, whom you will allow
to have merit, and who *had* more than he
has, I believe; how, I ſay, was he forced
upon inſignificant parts? I have ſeen his
name in the bills for *Don John*, in *Much
Ado about Nothing*.

What is urged as to my being under
Mr. Garrick's directions, with regard to improvement, is a very powerful argument
with me not to be with him. I have been
this two years labouring to loſe the reſemblance of him, which had like to have
ruined me for ever, and ſtamped me with
the diſgrace of mimickry, and now if I was

with

with him, I fhould *re*-gain all that would confirm that character to the world, and in my beft of praife fhould be called a very good *copy*. I fhall fee Mr. C——d after the play this evening, and then I will write more. I fhall ftipulate with Palmer, that I will play only on fuch nights as the company, I mean the gentry, are expected, and to re-linquifh fome certain characters, and only to engage from year to year. It is the opinion of my Lord Newnham, and many of my friends of that rank in life, that I ought not to go to London while Garrick is there.

I am but juft beginning to be talked of——Parties will, in time, be made in my favour by people of *rank* and *power*, but it muft be done by time—the protection and the influence of five or fix noblemen, will avail me more than any thing; however, I

have

have commiffioned Mr. C——d to nego-
ciate for me, fo far as to know Mr. Garrick's real intentions towards me, but on
no terms whatever will I confent to be liable
to infignificant characters. You cannot,
my dear Jack, you cannot imagine, how
foon I might be ruined in London, if I am
in the power of thofe who meditate my
ruin—for God's fake, only confider what an
irrecoverable fhock it would be to be obliged
to return to Bath, or to lay at the back of
the theatre on a falary of *bounty* more than
merit. As to Mr. Garrick's patronage and
friendfhip, I have no right to expect it. If
Mr. G—— had meant to patronize me, he
would have done it at *firft*, and not have
fent me to this place, which, though it was
as prudent a meafure as could be planned
for me, I really believe Mr. Garrick *did not
confider*. My reafons for this belief, are,
that he conftantly fpeaks in my difcredit, to

thofe

thofe whom he ever fpeaks to at all about me. A circumftance which you fhould con-fider maturely *as I have done.* The cafe is fimply this : I *have* great merit, or I *have not.* If I have, it fhould entitle me to a refpectable confideration. If I have *not,* I ought not to be feen in London, and lofe the fame I have there. Oh! but fay you and Mrs. I———, " Shandy, why will you be fo proud, there is a fecond rate fame and profit in the theatre, with which you fhould be content as yet"—I do not think fo. ————" Th' afpiring blood of Lancafter has not funk in the ground."†   My talents

are

† The letter, to which this is an anfwer, began with the following quotation :—

————" What !
" Will th' afpiring blood of Lancafter fink in the
       ground ?
" I thought it would have mounted."

are not of that caſt; though I have acquired great reputation in *Richard*, I ſhould make a very inſignificant figure in his good couſin of Buckingham. Hamlet too would ſup- port *me*, but I could never ſupport *Horatio*, and ſo on.

J. H.

To

To Mr. I———.

Bath, Jan. 2, 1775.

DEAR FRIEND,

IN confequence of the letter I told you I wrote to Mr. Garrick, upon which fubject alfo Mr. Taylor wrote, Mr. Garrick writes thus to Mr. Taylor.

" Dear Sir,

" I received laft night a letter from you,
" and another from Mr. Henderfon, upon
" the fame fubject—I fhall therefore beg,
" that this anfwer to you may ferve for both.
" In my opinion, your propofal would be
" a very injurious one to Mr. Henderfon—
" can he or you believe, that his playing

" only

" only twice, a different character too each
" time, would give the public a proper idea
" of his merit ?——The diffidence and ap-
" prehenfion, natural to a performer of feel-
" ing, might make him incapable of fhew-
" ing his talents and powers the firft time
" upon a new ftage, and upon which the
" great and eftablifhed eftimate muft be
" put upon his merit; fhould his fears
" prevail too much, which are ever ftrongeft
" with actors of keeneft fenfibility, he
" might be effentially hurt—could Mr.
" H. have an opportunity of performing
" ten or twelve different characters, his ge-
" nius would have fair play, otherwife, as
" his well-wifher, I proteft againft the
" other fcheme.   *   *   *   *

    *   *   *   *   *   *   *

    *   *   *   *   *   *.

M

" If

" If Mr. H. chufes to be with me,
" why fhould he not chufe three parts,
" Hamlet, Shylock, Benedick, or what he
" pleafes to appear in next feafon, and to
" have elbow room to difplay all his tra-
" gick and comick powers. I will either
" come into *certain* terms with him, or
" *conditional,* as he and his friends pleafe.
" I can fay no more, or offer any thing
" fairer, or more for his intereft.—I pro-
" teft againft the other partial manner of
" trial, which can be of no fervice to the
" manager, and may be of great prejudice
" Mr. Henderfon.

I am,

Dear Sir,

Yours, &c.

D. GARRICK."

Now, Jack, you know as much of the matter as I do.—What shall I do?—What proposals shall I make, and what answer shall I give?—You know very well, and so do all my friends, that the spirit of my design to stay in Bath was to make myself master of such a *number of principal cha-racters*, as would secure me from the danger of being employed in insignificant or improper ones; by *improper*, I mean such, as however important or reputable, do not come within the compass of my abilities; such for instance is Romeo, &c.—By being put into either, I conceive the little fame I have got would be ruined, and I should be in a much worse situation than if I had never ventured upon the stage. Mr. Garrick's letter indeed now seems to open me a security from that danger, and in my own mind I would leave to him *all other terms*, than those of *choosing my characters*.

I care

I care not how often I play, but Mr. Garrick may be led in his candour to imagine, I have succeeded in more characters than I really have.—Do, my dear Jack, lay this before my friends, and *consult and determine for me.* I say this not because I think your own decision insufficient, but because I hate to write the same letters to different people—there you see I have the honour to resemble Mr. Garrick.

J. H.

To

To Mr. I———.

Bath, January 23, 1775.

AS I find that lady has told you some cir-
cumstances about my negotiation with Mr.
Garrick, I now send you more. I wrote,
indeed, by the very next post, to desire her
not to acquaint you with any part of it 'till
she heard farther from me, because I had a
letter from Mr. C———d, which seemed to
open a new negotiation. I have not time to
copy it here, but its purport was, that *he*
wished the *past differences* might be forgot,
and the curtain dropped; I wrote in answer,
that " I was very willing to forget all that
had past, but that supposing the curtain *was*
dropped, the power of raising it, and open-
ing a new scene of negotiation, was not in
me; that, if through Mr. Cumberland's

M 3

means,

means, or by Mr. Garrick's own directions, any proposals were made to me, I would give a speedy and direct answer."

In consequence of this, I this morning received a letter, written by Mr. Garrick to Mr. C——d, wherein he says :—

" I cannot alter my opinion of Mr. H——n's proposals, but I say no more of them ; -- you seem to wish he should make his appearance upon our stage—As I have not seen him act, and cannot guess at his merit, which is so variously spoken of, I will agree that Mr. Henderson shall perform any two parts at the beginning of next season, which he shall please to fix upon, and afterwards upon others that we shall both agree upon. After he has performed ten or twelve times, and the public voice will be known, two gentlemen, one chosen

by

by him, and one by me, shall fix upon his
salary for the season; but, upon their dis-
agreement, a third may be called in, and
he must determine the difference.

" To make something certain for Mr.
Henderson and the referrees to go upon,
suppose we agree that his salary shall not be
less than *five* pounds a week, nor more than
ten, for the season, with a benefit. After
his salary is fixed, he must become like the
other performers, subject to my management *wholly*."

It will not be necessary to copy Mr.
C——d's letter to me—he advises the
scheme, and thinks I shall be *safe in the
experiment*.

Now, my dear Jack, you must know,
that *five* pounds a week in London, is not

much

much more than *four* pounds here, because *we* are paid every week, from the beginning of our feason 'till the end of it, alike; whereas in London, *all Lent*, and during thofe weeks in which the houfe is open only *three nights* in the week, the pay is but *half*.—Obferve, that Garrick only propofes to engage me one year, and at the end of that he might difgrace or lower me at his pleafure. If I ftay with Palmer, I engage for *three years*, and have three guineas a week—befides the advantage of the improvement that conftant acting of capital parts muft unavoidably give me.

Mr. Taylor is now in London, and I have juft had a letter from h'm, wherein he fays, after having feen Mr. Garrick play, " Depend upon it you will be received whenever Garrick retires from the ftage, with great *éclat*; I am more convinced of that *now*

than

than ever. It will not do for you to attempt rising on the stage as they do in the army and navy, by seniority; you must come out at once a comet, and not be content with appearing as a twinkling star, liable to be obscured by every little cloud that flies before you. To drop the metaphor, your talents must be so well improved and ripened, that any slight imperfections will be instantly overlooked, and your friends, the judges and true critics, be able to bear down the ill-natured remarks which will always attend true merit."

I am sure, my most dear, my most worthy friend, I shall impose a grateful task upon you, when I beg you to visit Mr. Taylor at his brother's house, and talk the matter over with him. I shall write by this post to prepare him for your visit, and afterwards fend me with all the fpeed you can, your opinion and advice.

You can have no conception of the anxiety of my mind in this affair. I dread London, I dread Garrick, I dread myfelf.

I truft you with all the vanities of my heart, and will therefore fend you the beginnings of thofe letters I made to you. You will fea by their dates how I addreffed you. There is no time, no hour hardly, in which I do not think of you with the fincereft and moft folicitous regard.

God blefs you—I have not time to correct what I have written.

J. HENDERSON.

With

With Henderson's conduct, in the course of the foregoing transactions, Mr. Garrick was highly offended; accused him of an insolent attempt to usurp his province, take the management out of his hands, and dictate such terms as no actor of the most established reputation had ever presumed to offer. This accusation Mr. Henderson warmly disclaimed; declaring, that the only motives which influenced him, were, that attention to his own fame which every man ought to preserve, and that attention to his own safety which the frequent conduct of managers to performers, gave some reason for; and which his duty to a public, who had honoured him by their approbation, to his friends, who had distinguished him by their partiality, and to himself, fully justified. This reasoning had no effect upon Mr. Garrick, and the hopes of an engagement at Drury-lane, were for the present

wholly

wholly given up.   But one of his friends, wishing him in a situation where his talents would have the encouragement they deserved, made application to Mr. Harris, who appeared pleased at the overture, and eager to engage him, which Henderson being informed, offered his services upon the same terms which had been prescribed by Mr. Garrick, and received for answer, that if he had any thoughts of continuing with Mr. Palmer, the London manager would by no means, come between them, whatever might be the eventual advantage to Covent-garden Theatre, and without waiting for an answer from Henderson, though he might possibly have heard from his friend Mr. Palmer, absolutely declined entering into any treaty with him, let the result of the Bath business, then pending, be what it would.

This .

This feemed to bar the door of Covent-garden Theatre, and his firſt determination was to quit Bath, and paſs a few months in France; but a prudent attention to his own intereſt, and the confequent timidity of mind, which dreaded being without an engagement, operated fo far, that he en-tered into a new agreement with the Bath manager.

To

To Mrs. I————

Bath, 24th Feb. 1775.

D I D not my narrative inform you that I had pofitively refufed ftaying with P————

————If you have not obferved it then, I do affure you now that *I have.* I fent it him in writing, and I will hold my promife to you and my friends,

I have not the leaft doubt but P————r hath obftructed my engagement at Covent-Garden,

" And will no doubt with reafons anfwer it,
" For Brutus is an *honourable man,*
" So are they *all, all honourable men."*

I certainly

I certainly will do as you advife, and
I think myfelf very happy that I have
fuch counfellors as I cannot oppofe without forfeiting all difcretion, or good fenfe.
—This is a ftrange turned phrafe, but I
take as much pains to avoid writing in
a ftrain of compliment to you, as fome
would to affect it, not becaufe *I* think
that civility and truth can be feldom united, for there again *you* act fo that there
is no feparating them, but that I would
not have you hum over thofe parts of my
letter as carelefs as you do thofe of any
other perfon, who celebrates your wit or
your good fenfe, or your good nature,
which I know you always think it better
to *poffefs* than to hear of.

Here you may take a pinch of fnuff.

I am

I am advised, on all hands, to pass this ensuing summer in France, in order to steal their receipt for making *incense*, and other materials, which, on my return, I may use on my theatrical altar, and make a solemn sacrifice to the *Graces*. This I shall certainly do; for though I know very well that all the ingredients may be bought in London, and cheaper too, than in France, yet I consider myself as a merchant who must obey the commissions of his correspondents, and send them whatever they demand from whatever shore they direct.

I assure you, my dear friend, that ever since I gave P———r a positive answer, my mind has been in constant serenity and composure.———I mean in all regards of future engagements, and I constantly reply, when any friends ask me how I can be so weak

as to throw myſelf out of all employment,
that I muſt take my chance, and I ſay it
with moſt unaffected indifference.

Pray have you ſeen my picture at Gainſborough's yet.—If not, why don't you go ?
—I intend it for my deareſt Jack, becauſe
I think it very like, and he who hath known
my heart for ſo many years, hath the beſt
title to my reſemblance.

I wiſh you had ſeen me play Hamlet
the other night.—*Vanity !*—Oh, you ſim-
pleton !——It was becauſe I ſhould have
ſeen *you here*.

If you make any more excuſes about
your writing, I will cut them out of your
letters, for they have no buſineſs there,
and ſend them back—beſides every excuſe
is an intruder, and takes up that room,

N   which

which I can prove by the other parts of your letters, would have contained much good humour and kindneſs and good writing, by which it is manifeſt you have cheated me; and it is an aggravation of your crime, that you have ſingled me out to impoſe upon from a large circle of people, who are all ready to ſwear that you never acted otherwiſe to them than with the moſt upright integrity. I repeat, that it is particularly cruel and unjuſt in you to treat me ſo, who am, as much as any of them can be for their ſouls,

Your very ſincere and faithful,

J. HENDERSON.

During the summer of 1775 he performed with Mr. Reddish at Bristol, where from the accidental indisposition of a performer, he on the seventeenth of August played Falstaff, a character which nature seemed to have forbade by every external disqualification. But the difficulty increased the honour, and success justified the undertaking.

It would degrade his memory, to compare him with any one who ever personated this *mountain of delight*, except Mr. Quin, who appeared mentally and corporeally formed for the character.

The first play I ever saw was Henry the Fourth, when Quin performed Falstaff, it being, I think, the last time he ap-

peared

peared on the ftage, for the benefit of Mr.
Ryan.

Of his playing I have not any recollection, but in the fcene of the battle,
inftead of the ftump of a tree on which
Falftaff fits to reft himfelf, I remember
the then directors of the Theatre introduced a crimfon velvet arm chair, with
gilt claw feet and blue fringe.

I have been told by thofe who have
a perfect remembrance of the veteran's
performance, that it was more important,
but lefs pleafant than Henderfon's, who
had alfo the fuperiority in the foliloquies,
but that where the old knight affumes
dignity, Quin's furly humour was beyond
competition.

In

In the summer of 1776, he played under
the management of Mr. Yates at Birmingham, and here first saw that meteor of the
drama, Mrs. *Siddons,* who, the preceding
season, had performed *Portia, Lady Anne,*
and a few other characters at Drury-Lane,
but with so little *éclat,* that upon Mr.
Garrick's retiring, the succeeding managers
not thinking her merits equal to a very
trifling salary, she was discharged for inability ! ! !

Of her talents Mr. Henderson entertained
the most exalted opinion, and wrote to Mr.
Palmer, recommending him in the strongest
terms to engage her, but he having already
a person under articles, who had a similar
cast of characters, the recommendation was
at that time without effect. Yet, who
that has seen Mrs. Siddons, will withhold
their sanction to Mr. Henderson's judgment.

It,

It may be almoſt ſaid of her, that, *as an actreſs*, ſhe has all the various merit which was poſſeſſed by any daughter of the tragic muſe who ever trod the Engliſh ſtage, and all the various merit which they wanted.

At the commencement of the ſeaſon he returned to Bath; a critique upon his per‑formance, under the ſignature of the Lon‑don Rider, appearing in the Morning Chro‑nicle, he notices it in the following letter.

To

To the Rev. Mr. D——.

Bath, November 7th, 1776.

Dear Friend,

I THANK you very heartily for your
letter; it confirms me in all that I have
thought of your candour and your friendſhip, which I have loved and honoured
ever ſince I was capable of loving and ho-
nouring any thing as I ought.——I wonder you ſhould think I was abuſed by the
London Rider, who, whatever his intentions
may be, has paid me the higheſt compliment.—His objections to me were, that I
imitated Garrick in *Sciolto,* and imitated
him in the worſt parts, his guttural ſounds,
&c.   Now it is certain I never ſaw Garrick

N 4   in

in Sciolto, and if I had, that thickneſs
and feebleneſs he complains of were not
improper for the *age* of Sciolto.——The
Rider doth not complain of thoſe defects
in Comus, in Lorenzo, in Falſtaff, which
certainly are not like Garrick's manner.
He only finds that they are, where I think
they ought to be, in an old and diſtreſſed
man.——He finds indeed that I have not dignity—he finds alſo that I have not gentility
enough for the gay Lorenzo, whom Elvira
is to fall in love with at the firſt ſight,
though I think he allows me ſome portion of eaſe and ſprightlineſs.——He finds
alſo that I have not an eye for the jocund
and voluptuous Falſtaff—I cannot help it,
but I have, without vanity, juſt ſuch an
eye as the *Poet* has aſſigned that character
——" Do you ſet down your name in the
" ſcrowl of youth," ſays the Chief Juſtice
to Falſtaff, " that are written down *old*,
with

with all the characters of age?—Have you not a *moist* eye?—a dry hand?—a yellow cheek?—a white beard?—a decreasing leg? —an encreasing belly? &c. &c. &c."——I believe by a *moist eye* is not there meant, that sparkling fluid which lends an appearance of penetration, and which gives point and expression.

But I am contented to want these requisites he says I have not, as long as I am thought to possess those he allows me ——But the London Rider should not decide so pointedly that I had better stay where I am——he has not seen many characters in which I succeed better than in those four he did see.

I have played, Doctor, since I have been upon the stage, which you know is only

four

four years, upwards of *seventy* characters, and most of them of the first importance, both for character and magnitude.—Judge if my faculties have not been pretty well stretched, and judge if I have not a claim to some indulgence on that score ——— I know you will be apt to say, it were better to have matured half a dozen, than to have run through such a number in the crude and hasty manner I must necessarily have done;—to which I answer, that this was not in my power. The people here will have variety, and our company is so limited, that the leaders in it are obliged to furnish out that variety from themselves; nor do I believe, that in the end it will hurt me. I wish Mr. Woodfall had chosen any other name to pay me his compliments in, than that of THE LONDON RIDER.

To

To ufe the language of Piftol,

> " Shall pack-horfes,
"And hollow-pamper'd jades of Afia,
" Which cannot go but thirty miles a day,
" Compare with Cæfars, and with cannibals,
" And Trojan Greeks ?"

I fincerely hope, my dear friend, that your happinefs is fecure, that Mrs. D—— and all your family are in health, and that they will continue fo, as I am really interefted in every thing that concerns you. Let me hear from you, and believe me truly,

Your's, &c.

J. HENDERSON.

The

The idea of playing at London was now
at an end, except some fortunate accident
should give him an introduction ; and this
accident happened when it was least expected.

Mr. Colman having, in 1777, purchased
from Mr. Foote the Patent of the Haymarket Theatre, engaged Henderson as a
performer, upon terms which will appear
by the following letter.

To

To Mr. I——.

January 8, 1777.

DEAR I——,

I HAVE agreed with Colman, and shall be at the Haymarket in the summer.

I am to play only my best characters, and I am to have an hundred pounds; besides, Colman has promised me his interest with the Chamberlain, to procure me a benefit after his patent closes, which, if I can compass, will be a very great thing for me; but I depend not upon that. I shall play Shylock first, I believe, but there is time enough to determine that—You can't conceive how I am in favour here—I

was

was at a mafquerade laft week, and got great credit.

Oh, Garrick and I are almoft reconciled; he has recommended me to Drury-lane. You may almoft be fure of my being at one of the theatres in London, when my time is out here. I do not yet repent my con-duct, nor have I reafon; but more hereafter.

My love to all your *familé*.

Your's, fincerely,

J. H.

To

To Mr. I———.

Bath, Feb. 12, 1777.

MY DEAR I——,

I HAVE juſt had my benefit, very brilliant, very crouded, and the beſt I have ever made in this place. I played Leon. I agree very much with you about Shylock; I will not make my firſt appearance in it, if I can prevail with Colman to alter his opinion, and I ſhall write to him for that purpoſe. However, it is proper that you ſhould know what that opinion was, and how it was grounded. He ſays, my manner of playing it is different enough from Macklin's to excite enquiry and examination, and he payed me the compliment to add, that he thought me ſufficiently grounded in the author to juſtify ſuch deviations, or dif-

ferences,

ferences, as there was from Macklin. He added also, that to make people talk and argue, and dispute, was what he aimed at, and seemed to be certain, that if he could do that, my reputation would be established by it. Now, though this is plausible and flattering to me, I think with you, that the popular spirit is too strong to be contested with at present, and therefore I propose, in my own mind, to begin more humbly, and rise, if I can, by degrees. I have made a figure lately in Valentine, in Love for Love, and Oakley in the Jealous Wife, and Leon. I will play as little tragedy as possible in the summer, for more reasons than one. The chief is, that I do not think myself ripe enough in the high tragic line; and another reason is, that tragedy will never be fol-lowed in the dog-days, except some extraor-dinary planet of attraction appears; and if I am neglected, I am ruined. I will play

Hamlet,

Hamlet, and *Richard the Third,* and *Shylock,* and perhaps *John.*

I am now ſtudying Henry the Fifth,
which, if I can make anſwerable to my
preſent ideas of it, I may perhaps add to
them, and I think no more. I ſhall have
infinite variety and ſcope in comedy, ſuch
as *Falſtaff, Bays, Don John, Benedick,
Leon, Oakley, Valentine, Felix,* &c. &c.

Richard the Second was once revived, but
the town would not bear it; there are no
women in it, and the whole play demands
the fineſt acting to make it pleaſing. By
the next poſt I ſhall take up the hundred
pound note I gave your brother H———.
Have not I been a good œconomiſt, and I
have paid near fifty pounds to J———n.

I am

I am happy to hear so well of Mortimer;
I do love that varlet; I hope he will continue as true to his own genius as that will
be to him. I hope too, that Gainsborough
will let you have my head—don't you think
it a very fine likeness.

My mother desires her best wishes may be
added to mine, for Mrs. I——— and yourself.
She is quite recovered:—Did I tell you,
we have changed our lodgings, and provide
for ourselves, and I market, and pur-
chase the tails of rabbits, and the beards
of oysters, and the heads and gizzards
of geese, for we leave their bodies to
the mighty ones of the earth, and I buy beef
steaks by the ounce, and have learnt to cut
up a shrimp most dextrously. In short, we
live upon the extremities of animals. I hear
the butcher's boy knock at the door with as
fine a sheep's tail in a tray as ever you saw
in your life—it is to be roasted, and if you

were

were here, you should have two joints out
of the five.

Adieu, we are very happy, and very truly
am I your friend, &c.

J. HENDERSON.

In cónfequence of Mr. Colman's engagement, he came to London, and on the 11th
of June 1777, begun his theatrical career in
the capital with the character of Shylock,
which, notwithftanding his own and his
friends objections, was the part the manager
introduced him in ; and the manner he per-
fonated the ferocious Jew, fully fatisfied the
propriety of Mr. Colman's choice.

I have been told, that previous to Mr.
Macklin's performance of Shylock, it was
looked upon as a part of little importance,
and played with the buffoonery of a Jew
pedlar ; to the underftanding of that vene-
rable performer, we are obliged for the firft
true reprefentation of the character ; but his
warmeft admirers will, I think, acknowledge, that though much fterling is left, he
fcarce acquired the reputation he enjoys in
the Jew, from his manner of now playing
it.

it. I know it will be deemed dramatic
herefy, but yet dare avow, that *I think*,
except in the fenate fcene, Henderfon performed it better than *I* ever faw Mr. Macklin. In that fcene, the judicious conception of this patriarch of the theatre, fe-
cures him from every competitor. He
praifed the young adventurer with great liberality for his *fpirited* performance; and,
on Henderfon's afferting, he had never had
the advantage of feeing him in the character,
replied, " Sir, it was not neceffary to tell
me that; I knew you had not, or you would
have played it very differently."

Teftimonials from authors to authors,
were, in the laft age, deemed neceffary em-
bellifhments to books, and as conftantly fubjoined as the *livelie pourtraiture of the pain-
fulle writer*. Teftimonials from players to
players, are not, I believe, very frequent.

 The

The following is the only one I ever heard Henderfon fpeak of having received; and, as I know he efteemed approbation from a gentleman of Mr. Digges' learning, experience, and judgment, as giving a fanction to his performance, I publifh it as a dramatic curiofity.

To

To Mr. HENDERSON.

Friday, twelve o'clock.

DEAR SIR,

I DID myself the pleasure of waiting on you this morning, to thank you for the uncommon delight I received in seeing your excellent performance of Shakespeare's Jew —I never saw a character more justly conceived, or more happily personated—I congratulate you on the great reputation you have established; a reputation you will rather augment than diminish—I think it a thousand pities you should be doomed to a provincial banishment, when you will be so much wished for in the capital. Permit

me

me to affure you, no perfon is more fenfible
of your merit, or will rejoice more in feeing
that merit rewarded, than,

Dear Sir,

Your moft obedient,

And moft humble fervant,

WEST DIGGES.

He afterwards performed Hamlet, Leon, Falſtaff, Richard, Don John, and Bayes. He was requeſted to play *Bays*, with imitations of the different actors, which, to the credit of his prudence, he re-fuſed.

During the very hot ſummer of 1777, the Haymarket Theatre was crouded. Mr. Henderſon being announced, operated as a charm : it attracted people of the firſt rank and taſte to a play-houſe in the dog-days.

Some of the diurnal critics praiſed him for merit he did not poſſeſs, but that the motive was to ſerve Mr. Colman, there appeared *a little reaſon* to ſuſpect, from the ſame conſiſtent gentlemen being

equally

equally lavish of their abuse, when
he played at Drury-lane. Of this un-
candid conduct he complains in the following letter.

To

TO MR. CUMBERLAND.

October 25th, 1777.

DEAR SIR,

I AM much obliged and honoured by your intelligence respecting the Battle of Hastings. I am ashamed to acknowledge, that I have not had an hour to myself of that kind that is fit to confider fo important a matter. One should neither be indolent nor fatigued, when a work of study is to be contemplated. Fatigued I have been to an extreme degree, * * * * *.

As soon as I have gone through the Roman Father, which I now have in rehearfal, I shall dedicate my studies to the Battle, and hope to revive the same pleaf-

ing

ing and magical ideas which I felt when you read it in Queen-Anne-ftreet.

I believe, my dear fir, you will agree that I have a moft difficult tafk to act.

The critics call out for novelty, for fpirit, for fire, for paffion, for every thing in fhort that they are taught by nature, or by reading to expect, and yet they are perpetually interrupting my emulation by the hopelefs profpect of ever attaining what they have been accuftomed to delight in, from Garrick, and Macklin. I have not the vanity to think myfelf equal, by many degrees, to either, but is it not hard they will not let me be what I am, nor by their good will let the people come and fee what that is.——I have the confolation of very good houfes indeed, or thefe gentlemen would make my theatrical life a very pain-

ful

ful one.——There are some public prints, that even call me names. I am honoured by one writer, who perhaps never saw me out of my dramatic dress, with the name of pragmatical puppy ; another, in insulting irony calls me a monster of perfection. But still I have good houses.——I am told my Richard is a despicable attempt at something, I know not what, but still I have good houses.

I am, &c.

J. HENDERSON.

Mr.

Mr. Colman having derived material advantage from his performer's popularity, difplayed great generofity at the end of the feafon. His conduct went "beyond the fixed and fettled rules," he gave Henderfon a *free benefit*, which produced upwards of two hundred pounds. He diftinguifhed him by every attention, and frequently invited him to his table, where Henderfon's delicacy and prudence once forfook him, for in the prefence of a large company he took off the manager's peculiarities to his face. I need not add that fo grofs an infult produced a coolnefs on the part of Mr. Colman.

The enfuing winter he was engaged by Mr. Sheridan to perform at Drury-Lane, at a falary of ten pounds a week, and a benefit. Before this could take place it was neceffary to fettle his forfeiture of three hundred pounds for the failure of his Bath articles.

articles. This, I believe, was done by Mr. Sheridan giving Palmer the liberty of exhibiting the School for Scandal, which was, I should suppose, at least an adequate compensation; added to this, it was stipulated that Henderson should perform a few nights at Bath, which he did.

He had an early contempt for *stage trick,* and one of the first times he played Hamlet at Drury-Lane, was so fully impressed with the spirit of the character, that in the closet scene, when describing the two miniatures, he whirled the king's picture from his hand. This was marked in one of the public prints as an innovation too violent for a young man. " Mr. Garrick never did it." The following night he checked his imagination, and kept possession of the picture. This was a fresh occasion for carping, and one gentleman, who I think

adopted

adopted the terrific fignature of *Scourge,* obferved, " that if right the firft night, he muft confequently be wrong the fecond," and added ; " In *our* opinion Mr. Henderfon departing from the eftablifhed cuftom of the Theatre, by fometimes neglecting to kick down the chair, on the appearance of the Ghoft, which was never omitted by the greateft actor who ever graced the ftage,* and not having always *got quit* of his hat, when he ftarts, in the firft fcene, is a violation of dramatic decorum, and deferves fevere reprehenfion from the critic. Deviations fo flight as to evade the common eye, and innovations fo trifling as to be thought unworthy of notice, have led the

way

* The chair in which Mr. Garrick fat, when he played in the clofet fcene, was fomewhat different from that appropriated to the queen, the cabriole feet being tapered, and placed fo much under the feat, that it fell with a touch.

way to herefies in religion, and the *abo-lifhment* of order in civil government. Let us nip error in the bud, and not by our filence give fanction to impropriety. Being once right, let us remain fo."

A friend of Henderfon's fent a reply to this curious rhapfody, which, being fhort, I fubjoin.

Two queries addreffed to the *fevere* SCOURGE.—Do you confider the Dramatis Perfonæ as *Automæa?* If you do, fhould not the magnificent Mr. Cox be manager, and that ingenious mechanift, Mr. Jaques Droz, prompter to your puppets? Thefe queftions were not anfwered.

On the fecond of January, 1778, he ap-peared in the character of Bobadil. Very high expectations were formed from the *éclat*

 with

with which it had been received at Bath.
But *there* it was an imitation of Woodward,
which would *here* have been deemed a burlefque of that moft excellent actor. Here,
I think, he failed, and, by endeavouring to
avoid Woodward's manner, departed from
the character.

I do not think myfelf at liberty to publifh
the name of the gentleman who wrote the
following letter. I know Mr. Henderfon
very properly thought himfelf honoured by
his regards, and frequently profited by his
judicious and friendly remarks.

To

Dublin, Nov. 13, 1777.

I SEE clearly, that you think I am not awake to your abilities, and that I am rather cold in your praife—I do affure you, you are miftaken—I know and feel your great fupe- riority to the prefent race of actors, and I have had, within thefe twelve months, fre- quent opportunities of declaring it. Mr. Garrick, and Mr. B. Sheridan, can teftify for me, that I ventured to *pronounce*, (that was the expreffion I made ufe of) before them, and Mr. Gibbon the hiftorian, laft winter, that you was an excellent performer in every thing, and capital in comedy. Thefe were my words, (which Sheridan and Gibbon, I dare fay, thought very pe-

P 2

remptory

remptory and affuming) but I was called upon by Mr. Garrick to declare my opinion as one which he relied upon, and Mr. Garrick immediately added his own fuffrage, and told Mr. Sheridan, that it was his bufinefs to fecure you as foon as poffible—I rather dwell upon this *literal* fact, becaufe Davies, in anfwer to my affertion, that Garrick had earneftly recommended you to Sheridan, fays abfurdly, that it was after fuch recommendation was *ineffectual*, and that you was obliged to wait 'till Sheridan had his own evidence of your powers and merit.

Here Davies grofsly miftakes; whether wilfully, or not, I am not fure, for Garrick recommended you whenever he could catch you. At the lateft, when your Bath articles fhould expire; and even then, Sheridan, in my prefence, talked of the fcheme

of getting you from Palmer, and fending
Grift to Bath.   This Mr. Garrick and I
both approved of — * * * * * * * *
* * * *.   ·

As to newfpaper puffing, (which Davies
is fo fond of) it is the foolifheft thing in
the world, becaufe it produces all thofe cri-
ticifms which you allude to.   As to converfation puffing from good authority, I
think quite otherwife of it—The generality
of the world are much led by their own
circle; but newfpaper commendation is uni-
verfally confidered as the advertifement of a
quack doctor.   I faw in one paper, Benfley
preferred to you in Horatius.   I have not
feen your Horatius, but I *have* your Al-
canor, and I am fure your Horatius muft
be good.

                          Lucius

Lucius Junius Brutus, and the Battle of Haftings, have been promifed places in this feafon for more than a year paft—Shirley, I believe, for years.

As to the Law of Lombardy, the author thinks the parts are equal. I differ from him widely. There is a young gallant knight driven to a defpair of jealoufy, by the villainous acts of a plotting rival. They fight in the end, and are the confpicuous men; but the perfon worked upon I always think a better part than the worker. I go fo far as to think Alonzo a finer character than Zanga. Polidore muft be the favourite. He is *Pofthumus*, if poffible, more impaffioned. This being the caft, which you feemed to me to decline, I naturally looked at the other character for you. But nothing is, or can, be yet fettled about it. There is an old king, and father alfo,

that

that requires an excellent actor ; *that*, I con-
clude must be crucified, as the fine part of
Almada was.

As for your search for new readings, I do
not like them. Your restoration of good
passages I can never disapprove of. That
in Richard I like very well. * * * * *
* * * * * * * *,

To return to your innovations—I cannot
see, how changed readings, and points, are
in any sort connected with the stile of
acting. It is introducing criticism into
acting, which I think never should be ;
and if it should be bad criticism (such
as the croaking raven) what can be said
for it ?

I hear

I hear your laboured ſhew of propriety much condemned—But all theſe remarks are to your honour. They would not be made, but that you are confeſſedly at the head of the ſtage.

Your ſincere

And obedient ſervant,

E. T.

You ſay all your novelties are defenſible; if I thought ſo, I ſhould not blame you for them—You aſk me, if you have ever ſpoiled the ſenſe—I think groſsly in the *croaking raven*, if you ſpeak it as my reporter informs me.

In the summer of 1778 he went to Ireland.   His reception from that generous
people, is described in the following letter.

To

To Mr. I———.

Dublin, 5th June, 1780.

No, my dear boy, I am as well as I ought to expect, though my arms, at least one of them, are troublesome. The true reason of my not writing is, that I am half ashamed to tell you the consequences of my expedition, but I now find that I ought not to impute it to my own weakness of fame or talent, but to the universal distress and poverty this kingdom at present labours under.

The first character I played, was Hamlet, and carried hence no more than fourteen pound three shillings, though the Lord Lieutenant did me the honour of his presence.

fence. The next night I voluntarily and chearfully gave to a charity for the diftreffed manufacturers : it was Falftaff—not five pounds in the galleries, nor above feventy in the whole houfe; a ftrong inftance of their inability upon fo good, fo ufeful an occafion. My third character was Shylock, and there was not expences in the houfe.— This night I fhall play Richard.—I have given up all thoughts of getting any thing, except by a benefit, which I have reafon to hope will be handfome, for I cannot defcribe to you how I am careffed by the people of fafhion, the only few who can go to a play. The Duke of Leinfter does me every kindnefs imaginable. I was laft night at the Caftle, at the ball and fupper. More than a hundred people of rank and fafhion, and tafte, defired to be made known to me.—In fhort, more flattery, more at-tention, and confequently more happinefs,

I never

I never tasted—my spirits have been in one state of the most delicious delirium ever since I touched this shore.—I have no time though, for it is the custom here to wait upon strangers, and my lodgings are crouded when I am at home.—Except lodgings it has not cost me a shilling since I came to this place, nor would it if I were to stay here this six months.—I am very glad I came, because it will extend my connections and my fame, though it may not be very advantageous to my purse. I intended to have written a whimsical account of my voyage; we were forty hours upon the water, but I was not sick above two hours the whole time, and that moderately.——I don't know what my friend E—— has done for me, nor when I am to quit this place. Whenever I do, it will be with reluctance—but if it will not take up too much of his time, I should like to know about it.

Mrs.

Mrs. Barry is here, but she finds the condition of the people, and I believe will not play, if she does I will make safe conditions for myself. I am to have ten guineas a night, and if the house amounts to a fixed sum, fifteen. But my benefit is my only object.

J. H.

Thanks for the Plays.

After

After his return from Ireland, on the 13th of January 1779, the writer of thefe anecdotes had the honour of prefenting to him, that beft of all good gifts a wife, * and the following year, as fponfor, gave the name of Harriet to a daughter, who, by the death of her father, has loft not only a protector, but an inftructor very capable of forming and improving her mind,

Among other characters new to him in the metropolis, he performed King John.

One of his friends wrote him a few remarks, which I have fubjoined, as I think there are fome fenfible ftrictures upon his playing.——The advice at the conclufion, that

* She was daughter to Mr. Figgins, of Chippenham in Somerfetfhire.

that " when preparing for a new part he
fhould retire to his own room, &c." was
founded upon the writer's having obferved
Mr. *Henderfon's mode of preparation*, which
was almoft invariably this. When a new
part was appointed him, he firft read the
play : I mention this, becaufe I have
heard the practice is not univerfal among
the dramatis perfonæ. He then imprinted
the words of the character he was to per-
fonate upon his memory, which, to him,
was not a very difficult tafk ; looked over
the play flightly a fecond time, and then
laid it afide, and though this ceremony
was frequently gone through a fortnight
before the performance, feldom looked at
it again.—The evening before his appearance, was ufually preceded by a hearty
dinner, a chearful, but moderate glafs of
wine, and a game at cribbage, which

was

was almost always his amusement until a few minutes before the curtain drew up, and he was obliged, sometimes very unwillingly, to appear at the Theatre.

To

To Mr. Henderson.

DEAR HENDERSON,

I LAST night sat by Kenrick during the play, in the front boxes—I had a good deal of converfation with him—He feemed not unwilling to do juftice to your merit, but complained of your method of toning your voice; by copying Garrick's under-play, he faid you were fcarce intelligible to the audience—I affured him that he was greatly miftaken, for that you had not very often feen Garrick, nor could you copy his King John, which Garrick had not acted for thirty years paft. However, he was fo far right that you apparently wanted fpirit, and your voice was lower and more indiftinct than the crack'd pipkin of the king

of France.——You loſt opportunities of getting applauſe· with Pandolph, you gave
little or no force to the popular, as well as
juſt ſentiments of an Engliſh king, diſ-
daining to be governed by an Italian prieſt
——Your action was extremely confined and
ſpiritleſs—your general idea of the raſcal
John, who compared to Richard is as a
foot-pad, or pick-pocket, oppoſed to a
highwayman, was juſt; your ſcene with
Hubert was well planned, and maſterly,
though you was rather too low—I never
loſt a word of your's 'till laſt night—Kenrick obſerved that you wanted variety—In
the dying ſcene, you made ample amends
for all deficiencies in the foregoing acts—
Kenrick owned you was excellent.

And now let me remind you, of your
neglecting to give due fire and ſpirit to that

excellent

excellent scene of John with Hubert in the fourth act—your reproaches lost all effect with the audience from under-play, or taking your voice too low.   You suffered Hubert to make the most of that passionate interview, and to rob you of the applause you would have merited by a proper exertion of your powers.—I told K———— that I fancied you was not well, or at least not in spirits.

Believe me I do not aim to teach or direct you, who know so much more of the matter than I can pretend to, but the less skilful stander-by can see defects in a very able gamester.

I would recommend your imitation of Garrick in one part of his conduct: whenever he had a new or capital character to act, he saw no company that day, and dined

alone

alone upon a trifling difh. This was his conftant practice, I believe from his firft treading the ftage 'till he left it.

On fuch an occafion as acting a new part, &c. I would after dining with Mr. and Mrs. I———, retire to my own room, nor would I be difturbed by any vifitor whatfoever.— I tell you again and again, you will deftroy both voice and ftomach by your curfed hot fippings—excufe my freedom,

Yours, ever,

T. D.

Saturday eleven o'Clock.

The fat parfon G——— is juft gone paft to preach a charity fermon.

In confequence of this letter and fome other advice, he once changed his cuftom, retired to his chamber and ftudied his part on the day of playing. The confequence was a coldly correct, and moft vapid perform-ance, which convinced him and his friends that his firft practice was right, at leaft for him.—He ferioufly vowed no earthly power fhould induce him to repeat the experi-ment, adding, at the fame time, that he thought it poffible, that a number of very grave men, who muzzed away much time alone in their own apartments, were quite as likely to be fleeping as ftudying.

During the time he performed at Drury-Lane, Mr. Sheridan the elder, very properly confidering his peculiar excellence in fpeak-ing tales, fables, or any light airy compofi-tion, revived Sir John Vanbrugh's Æfop, with fome alterations, which, from having heard

Q 3 Henderfon

Henderſon read it, I think he would have made a moſt popular and entertaining character. He entered with true humour into the ſpirit of the little tales, and gave full force to the *Cervantic* gravity of the old moraliſt. But the town were too faſtidious to ſuffer the performance in even its altered ſtate, Mr. Yates perſonated a country ſquire, a character the preſent age know only from deſcription ; the ſavage preferred his hounds to his wife, and Æſop was driven from the ſtage,

Among thoſe who moſt violently inſiſted upon its being withdrawn, were ſome of the critical leaders of the taſte of the town, who conſidered, and perhaps with good reaſon, that ſhould it ſucceed, the fabuliſt might be made a vehicle to anſwer the diurnal remarks which ornament our

daily

daily papers, and therefore very prudently silenced him the firſt night.

In the ſummer of 1779 he returned to Dublin, and was gratified by every mark of attention, noticed by people of diſtinction, and received, not merely as an actor, but a companion, by families of the firſt conſequence.

The annexed letter is one example, among many others, of the reſpect with which the gentlemen of Ireland, diſtinguiſh and protect genius, in any ſituation.

Mr. Gardiner's teſtimony is ſo high an honour to Henderſon's memory, that I ſhould not be juſtified in withholding it. I hope,—I believe,—the ſame liberality of ſentiment which dictated ſuch a letter, will pardon its inſertion.

Copy

Copy of a Letter from Mr. Gardiner to Lord Doneraile.

Black-Rock, *July 6th,* 1779.

My DEAR LORD,

AS Mr. Henderson is going to Cork to perform there, I thought I could not do him a greater service than to recommend him to your attention. He has given us much entertainment here, and I doubt not will afford you equal pleasure in the line of his profession. I have had frequent opportunities of being in company with him and Mrs. H. and have found them so agreeable, that I need make no apology for introducing them to your lordship's acquaintance,

particularly,

particularly, as such talents as his, united with good humour, and good breeding, are at this day peculiarly rare.

I remain, &c.

J. GARDINER.

The

The enfuing feafon Mr. Sheridan and Henderfon difagreed upon terms, the expectations of the latter being higher than the manager thought proper to comply with; what thofe expectations were founded upon, are defcribed as follows.

To

To Mr. I————.

Dublin, June 29, 1779.

I WAITED for something of more importance than our safe arrival to inform you
of, and now I have a subject. The principal people are so desirous of my wintering
here, that they have made me the most flattering, the most honourable proposals. To
secure me from the *accidents* (ACCIDENT
is here a word of great pith and moment,
and used for safety, because letters may be
mislaid) which may happen in a negotiation
with the Irish manager; they will raise a
subscription among themselves, and the Lord
Lieutenant himself offers a hundred guineas
towards it; the rest will amount to a larger
sum than I should receive in England, even
if my demands were complied with, and I

consider

confider the houfe in Buckingham-ftreet as untenanted, and pay the rent myfelf. Now I am in a ftate of moft tormenting fufpenfe; for I hear nothing either from the elder, or the younger Sheridan—They feem to have no great earneftnefs in their wifh that I fhould continue with them, and yet I do not care to ftay here, unlefs they pofitively anfwer me, *yes* or *no.*

This place is poor beyond all names of poverty, at leaft fo the people fay, and I am fure the Theatre bears the marks of it; but if I ftay, I depend upon thofe who cannot be poor in any country. Mrs. Crawford certainly ftays here, and I fhall have the advantage of playing with her. C——d is abominated by the critics, and all people here are critics. I am now going to Corke, fo that you muft direct to me there. If you would fee the elder Mr. Sheridan, and

learn

learn from him what I am to do, I should be glad. I dare not send him the proposals that are made me at large, lest it should be construed an artifice to raise my confequence in England, or a treachery to the proprietors here. But something I muft do, and speedily.

Whether the propofals here are accepted or not, nothing can be more favourable to my reputation, than their having been made by people of fuch rank, and tafte, and importance, as they are.

Adieu, my deareft friend,

Affure yourfelf, I am moft affectionately,

Your's, &c.

J. HENDERSON.

To Mr. I————.

July 16, 1779.

THE very day that I wrote to you, I wrote also to the elder Sheridan ; I told him my offers, and gave him 'till the firſt of Auguſt to determine. I ſhall not recede from my claims, as I think them juſt.

I yeſterday received a letter from the treaſurer of Drury-lane, acquainting me, that he was ordered by the proprietors, ten days before, to write to me, and to inform me that they were ready to treat with me upon the ſame terms as laſt year. I have no doubt that this was written in conſequence of mine to S————, and that *the ten days* is a lye. This letter I anſwered, by ſaying, that Mr. Sheridan, the elder, was ac-

quainted

quainted with my refolutions, and that I
fhould be governed by his anfwer, which I
fhall, and by the firft of Auguft I fhall
decide. Nothing is more likely, than that
S—— would wifh to be the hero: he probably wifhes it, and it may probably happen.
I do not fee, my dear lad, what you can
do; I muft wait his reply, and act accord-
ingly. At all events, it is an honourable
retreat for me, and I may be more wanted
another year. I muft write more at large,
when I know more, and have more time.

J. H.

To

To Mr. I———,

Cork, Aug. 24, 1779.

DEAR JACK,

MY letter to E—— ſtates all my deſigns,
and I need not repeat them to you. When
you have read the letter will you ſend it?
I write to E——, becauſe I would have it
ſhewn to Sheridan; and I am reſolved to
adhere to my terms. I can make a very
handſome bargain here, and complete it in
three months. I ſhall get more money, and
be leſs a ſlave, and eſcape the unworthy
treatment I have found in London. I feel
my own importance more than ever I did,
and I will not be trampled on. Pray, my
dear boy, copy, or get this letter copied,
for I have not time, and learn, if you

can,

can what answer he gets, and write to
me at Birmingham.   I do not urge *him*
to an answer; becauſe it looks like too
much anxiety.

                            J. H.

To Mr. E————.

Aug. 24, 1779.

Dᴇᴀʀ E——,

YOU will, perhaps, be difappointed when I decline Mr. Sheridan's offer, but you ought, of all people, to be the leaft fo, becaufe you muft remember the converfation you was prefent at, between Mr. S—— and myfelf, when I made my firft agreement with him. You remember, that my falary was no more than ten pounds a week, becaufe my forfeiture was urged, and you remember Mr. Sheridan urged that forfeiture being *equally* paid, whether in *money*, or in *property*. You remember alfo, that Mr. Sheridan urged, that I fhould be moderate in my firft claims, and *rife*, by degrees, in the Theatre, and now he propofes that I

fhould

ſhould ſink in it ; for fifteen guineas a week
is not more than I had, computing my forfeiture, and I ought in juſtice to have ranked
in the Theatre agreeable to *that* ſalary,
though, in the quietneſs of my diſpoſition, I
forbore a claim which might be troubleſome
without material advantage; My reception
in this kingdom, among ſuch perſons as it
is moſt an actor's honour as well as intereſt
to pleaſe, has not moderated my opinion of
the juſtice of my claim, to an equal ſalary,
and equal rank, with Mr. Smith. When
I converſed with the elder Mr. Sheridan in
the Park, he told me, that Mr. S———, his
ſon, could not deny the reaſonableneſs of
my claim, but that, for certain reaſons; it
could not be complied with for the next
ſeaſon ; that if I would ſtay on my preſent
ſalary for one year more, I ſhould have my
demands in future. To this I anſwered,
agreeable to my deſire of accommodation, &c.

R 2

that

that if he would give me twelve guineas per week *now*, and fifteen guineas a week in a future season, I would be content. If Mr. Sheridan had made me *that* offer now, I believe I should have closed with him, but I cannot accept his twelve pounds, and no assurance of rising the next season. I could have contented myself with postponing my claim, but am not content to relinquish it.

I have received a letter from Mr. T. S. in which he tells me, that the patentees are determined to raise no salaries, and yet I am assured, that an actor, with whom it would do me no very great honour to be compared, has obtained an encrease of his. I know very well, how little force, arguments and reasons have with managers, and, therefore, I do not use them there; but this is, my friend, to justify myself to you—Whilst I

feel

feel no diminution of my own powers, nor any decline of the public approbation, I fee no reafon why I fhould humble myfelf to the difadvantage of my intereft, or my importance in a Theatre.—My defign, therefore, is to fet off for England, play a few nights at Birmingham, proceed to London; from thence return to Ireland about December, which will be time enough to compleat entirely the plan I have in meditation, and to anfwer all my defigns. I fhall be in Buckingham-ftreet, I hope, by the latter end of September, unlefs I find it convenient to perform longer in the country. I hope you will not condemn me for not accepting Mr. Sheridan's offer, nor think I am at all in exile. Why fhould I leave a place where I am careffed by all ranks of people, to accept terms that degrade me from my firft conditions, and keep me inferior to thofe whom the public do not prefer to me.—I

muft

muſt remind you, that the conditions on which I ſtay here, are ſuch as, I believe, have not happened to any other actor, and, therefore, muſt do me honour in the world. I may, poſſibly, paſs my next ſummer in London to great advantage, as well as con-venience; in the mean time, I will not weakly embrace the fetters which the London coalition are forging for us. It requires no very great foreſight to obſerve the toils which are gathering round us. I thank God, I need not at this period ruſh into them, and, therefore, I feel eaſier than when I left England.

I am, &c.

J. H.

P. S.   In order that my terms may be fully underſtood, I repeat to you, that I ſhould

ſo

fo far compromife the matter, to accept
of twelve guineas for the next feafon,
and fifteen for the two fucceeding—But
I cannot play for twelve, without an af-
furance of the reft.

At

At the commencement of the winter 1779, he removed to Covent Garden, at a falary of twelve pounds a week, and performed feveral characters, new to him, with encreafed reputation — Macbeth, for the firft time at this Theatre, on the 18th of October.

When he appeared with the daggers after the murder of Duncan, I think the countenance of horror and remorfe which he affumed, was equal to any exhibition I ever faw upon the ftage, and much critical knowledge of the character was difplayed through the whole; yet in the other fcenes he wanted the fpeaking terrors of Mr. Garrick's look and action, which can no more be defcribed than they can be equalled.

The fummer of 1780 he paffed at Liverpool. To fay he was well received, will

be

be a repetition of that which has been already said, but, furely, the actor who has powers of attraction fufficient to induce men of fcience to come from diftant parts of a province to be prefent at his performance, muft be allowed to derive fome honour from their attendance; efpecially when it is confidered, that province was Lancafhire; for it will not be eafy to find any country fo eminently diftinguifhed for the liberality and fcientific knowledge, of thofe who have been, and are its inhabitants.

In the winter he returned to Covent-Garden. Among other characters he performed Wolfey. His fenfible fpeaking and accurate elocution marked the character, but in fome of the fcenes he wanted that dignity

which

which the poet and hiſtorian* (for an hiſtorian our immortal dramatiſt may be called) has given to the haughty Cardinal.

He played Sir John Brute, and I thought pleaſantly, but Mr. Garrick obſerved, " it was the city Sir John, for egad he had neither the air nor the manner of the rake of faſhion."

I believe it was in this ſeaſon he firſt perſonated Iago, a character in which perhaps he has not been equalled. A very good idea of the manner in which he

looked

* A writer of ſome eminence ſays, that the great Duke of Marlborough was ignorant of Engliſh hiſtory, and to prove his aſſertion, gives an inſtance of his Grace having once quoted Shakeſpeare, as an authority upon a diſputed point. The inſtance was ſurely unfortunate.

looked it, may be formed from Bartolozzi's engraving; when I add it was from a ſketch by Stuart, *though at only one ſitting,* 'tis ſcarce neceſſary to ſay it exhibits a moſt ſtriking reſemblance.

Sir Charles Eaſy he played for a benefit. The character ſat heavy upon him. I remember Foote uſed to tell of an eminent actor of the old ſchool, who being informed he muſt play Richard the Third, the following night, returned for anſwer to the manager, " that his rheumatiſin was ſo bad he could ſcarcely ſtir hand or foot, but if they would get up the Careleſs Huſband, he was ready to play *Sir Charles Eaſy,* inſtead of the king."

Finding it impoſſible to make his own terms in the ſummer of 1781, he had not any Theatrical employment, except that he

one

one night played Falstaff at the Haymarket, for the benefit of Mr. Edwin.

His hours of leisure he frequently employed in copying old plays, and I verily
believe it was upon these occasions only,
that he read them, for no man had less
reverence for the BLACK LETTER than
Mr. John Henderson. His opinion of
large libraries was not much more favourable. He used to quote the remark
of somebody, who said, " that most
men who got together vast quantities of
books, put him in mind of the Italian
finger who founded a Seraglio." I believe,
in general, the greatest collectors are not
the most remarkable for being the deepest
readers. Indeed the time taken up in hunt-
ing after *scarce books*, does not leave much
learned leisure for perusing them.

In the summer of 1782 he played at Liverpool, where I think his benefit amounted to nearly two hundred pounds.

In the winter he performed Lusignan, but his powers were unequal to either that or Lear. The pathetic was not his *forte*, had he been left to the choice of his own characters, I believe he would no more have played Lear than Romeo. He thought highly, and not unjustly of his own merit in speaking the Chorusses to Henry the Fifth, which being rather an unpopular play, he did not, I believe, appear in after January 1779, when I saw him. His figure acquired grace from the Vandyke habit. His recitation led me to regret it was not repeated. He was accurate, animated, energetic.

In the November of 1783 he appeared in Tamerlane, to Mr. Kemble's Bajazet; but the fire of the tyrannic Bajazet predominated over the tame Tamerlane, who, notwithſtanding the avowed intention of the poet, was to give a ſemblance of, and pay a compliment to, our third William, is a vapid, heavy, and inſipid part.

The ſummer of 1784 he paſſed at Edinburgh, and it was obſerved, that the *Reverendi,* and *Reverendiſſimi,* laid aſide their ancient prejudices*, and appeared in a playhouſe, to behold Mrs. Siddons, and Mr. Henderſon.

* Theſe prejudices were not peculiar to Scotland; the ſame narrowneſs of ſentiment pervaded a numerous claſs of people in this kingdom, not very many years ago. On a ſet of itinerants being once tolerably well received at Kidderminſter, in Worceſterſhire, a Mr. Watſon nailed a card, with the following lines, upon

Henderſon. How different were the ſentiments of this people in the days of that ſevere ſcourge of diſſipation, John Knox, when the repreſentation of a play would have excited horror, and the whole company had been devoted to deſtruction, as a regiment under the banner of the woman of Babylon.

During

the door of the barn where they enacted, which was dignified with the name of, *The Summer Royal Theatre.*

" How art thou fallen, oh ! Kidderminſter ;
" When every ſpulſter, ſpinner, ſpinſter,
" Whoſe fathers liv'd in † Baxter's prayers,
" Are now run gadding after players :
" Oh ! Richard, couldſt thou take a ſurvey,
" Of this vile place, for ſin ſo ſcurvy,
" Thy pious ſhade, enrag'd would ſcold them,
" And make the barn too hot to hold them."

† Richard Baxter, who was very many years minister of that place.

During the summer of 1785, he performed a few nights at Dublin, and was honoured by an invitation to the Castle, where he read the story of Le Fevre, and some other select passages, from his favourite Sterne, to the Duke and Dutchess of Rutland, and their court.

In the Lent season, Mr. Sheridan and he united in public readings at Freemasons Hall. The terms were thought high, but justified by success. The opinion entertained of them by the public, may be gathered from the crouds who attended every night during their continuance, and from the sum which was gained; I think not less than eight hundred pounds. Having in a former page given my opinion of his performance, I need not repeat it. He however read into reputation some things which

seemed

feemed to have been gathered to the dull
of ancient days, and but for fuch a revival
had probably been ftill covered with the cloak
of oblivion.* Had Mr. Henderfon lived,
this entertainment would have been continued, as he requefted from a gentleman eminent for his tafte and judgement,† a felec-
tion from thofe writers moft likely to be
popular.

Previous to his voyage to Dublin, fome
little differences between Mr. Harris and
him had been accommodated, and he renewed
an engagement for four years, I have been
told, at feventeen, eighteen, nineteen and

S

twenty

---

* *One* Printfeller fold 6000 copies of John Gilpin's
Race, which had been feveral years before printed in
one of the public papers, but fcarcely noticed.

† Mr. Caleb Whitefoord.

twenty pounds a week.   But his laſt performance was Horatius in the Roman Father, on the third of November, 1785.

He was ſoon after ſeized with a diſor-
der which ſeemed to have ſubmitted to me-
dicine, but when his complaints put on
the moſt favourable appearance, a ſudden
death deprived the public of an excellent performer, and his friends of an agreeable
companion, on the 25th of November, 1785,
in the 40th year of his age.

An eminent ſurgeon gives the following
account :

" Henderſon's liver was entirely undi-
ſeaſed ; the lungs in perfect health ; the
brain had no extravaſation, whatever to external appearance.   His ſtomach was pre-
ternaturally ſtrong.   His heart was the only

part

part of the fyftem which failed. His heart was literally broken, that is, it had loft its accuftomed firmnefs of tone. It is by far the ftouteft mufcle in the human body, and the leading veffels were all offified, or offifying. In fhort, if I had not known Mr. Henderfon, and feen his face, his teeth, and his hair, I fhould have fuppofed from his heart, that his age had been ninety."

On the third of December following, he was interred in Weftminfter Abbey, near Doctor Johnfon and Mr. Garrick, the chapter and the choir attending to pay refpect to his memory. His pall was fup-ported by the honourable Mr. Byng, Mr. Malone, Mr. Whitefoord, Mr. Stevens, and Mr. Hoole.

I have

I have not feen any epitaph to his memory, nor is it eafy to write one properly defcriptive of his profeffion.

" The Actor only, fhrinks from time's award;
Feeble tradition is his memory's guard;
By whofe faint breath his merits muft abide,
Unvouch'd by proof—to fubftance unallied !"

The moft concife Epitaph I recollect to
have feen upon a player, was

Exit Burbage.

From the time of his *entré* on a London ftage, he was overwhelmed with in-
difcriminate and ill judged flattery. This
might ferve the manager, but injured the
player, and inflated the man.

It fo far kindled the embers of vanity in
his mind, as to demand the full exercife of

his

his underſtanding to keep them from a blaze. It called forth critical oppoſition, which ſometimes produced too ſevere a ſcrutiny.

His death has embalmed his name, ſince that time we have had, not characters, but echoing plaudits. Profeſſing to deſcribe what Henderſon was, they tell you what a player and a man ought to be.

Such eulogies diſplay the ingenuity of the writer, but do not much ·ſanctify the object of their adulation.

They have enveloped his character in the miſt of panegyric, and in their zeal to con-ſecrate his memory have forgotten that ex-ceſs of decoration diſguiſes and deſtroys the reſemblance, of thoſe it is intended to dig-

S 3

nify;

nify ; for to all the defcriptions of him which I have feen, it was neceffary to infcribe the name, or I fhould never have fufpected fuch high coloured pictures were intended as portraits of Henderfon.

Abfolute perfection is not the lot of humanity, and after all the fine things which have been faid, his relative merit is the criterion by which he muft be tried, nor will that merit fuffer much diminution by being oppofed to thofe with whom he was cotemporary.

If it fhould be thought I am too minute, I can only anfwer, that when reading of a man who was eminent, I have ever wifhed to know what were his peculiar difpofitions, and domeftic habits, by what qualities he attracted attention, and what were the methods by which he acquired reputation.

By

By some it may be thought that I over-rate his abilities, and there may be those who will think I have not allowed him all that he possessed. In the delineation of a man's person, or disposition, I consider likeness to the original as the leading excellence, and that I have attempted in the following

CHARACTER.

As an actor he had many disadvantages to cope with. His height was below the common standard. He had an uncompacted frame. His limbs were ill proportioned; they were too short; he had not much of that flexibility of countenance which anticipates the tongue, that language of the eye which prepares the spectator for the

coming

coming fentence, enchains attention, and en-
fures partiality.*

His voice wanted the melifluous filver
found which charms the ear, and was deficient in that dignified ftrength which commands refpect. It was not fuited to the
foftnefs of love, where the very found produces fympathy, nor to the wild rage of
tyranny, which awes the multitude.

But the ftrength of his judgment, and
the fervency of his mind, broke through
the mounds which nature feemed to have
placed between him and excellence.

His

* He frequently faid, " Whenever he threw meaning
into his eye, *it was from fomewhat which lay behind it,*
for he was confcious, *naturally,* it was heavy, and deftitute of expreffion." In the hours when his countenance was lighted up, it bore a ftrong refemblance to
a portrait of Betterton, by Sir Godfrey Kneller, in the
poffeffion of Mr. Samuel Ireland.

His comprehension was ample, his knowledge diverfified, and his elocution accurate,

Where fenfible recitation was the leading feature of a character, he had no fuperior. In the varieties of Shakefpeare's foliloquy, where more is meant than meets the ear, he had no equal.

In that fpecies of eloquence, he difcriminated with peculiar propriety the melancholy Jacques, and the penfive Hamlet, the whimfical Benedick, and the voluptuous Falftaff. In the whole of that part he was without a competitor, and not having left any lawful fucceffor, the humour of the fat knight muft be confined to the clofet.

Being little acquainted with fencing, or dancing, his deportment was neither eafy

nor

nor difengaged, and in fcenes where the former accomplifhment was neceffary, appeared to great difadvantage. Sometimes. the fuperior fkill of his opponent ftruck the fword from his hand, at the moment which required its firmeft grafp—yet the character of Hamlet, he fuftained with fuch tafte, feeling, and propriety, that we forgot every light imperfection ; and, except when he would faw the air with rather too much famenefs, he approached very near perfection. His manner of fpeaking three words, " *The fair Ophelia !*" ftill vibrates upon my ear. It was equal to Mrs. Crawford's, *was he alive?* Superior it could not be.

In the inftructions to the players, it will not be violating truth, to fay, he excelled Mr. Garrick. In one, we faw the Manager ; in the other, the Prince of Denmark.

His

His range was extensive, especially in
comedy. I do not so much mean in the
number of parts, as their opposition of
character*.

In the flimsy declamation of modern tragedy, he added little to his reputation.
Shakespeare was the deity he worshipped,
entered into the spirit of the characters, as
drawn by that mighty master of the human
heart, and feeling with enthusiasm, exhibited
them with ardour. Yet to some he was
unequal ; and who has been able to personate all the creations of a Shakespeare's
boundless fancy ?

He

* To instance a few. What can be more dissimilar
than Iago and Benedick ; Hamlet and Falstaff ; Shylock
and Posthumus ; Jaques and Don John ; Brutus and
Comus ; Cardinal Wolsey and Sir John Brute ; Leon
and Sir Giles Overreach.

He had moſt uncommon powers of imitation, and gave, with the voice and geſture,
the countenance, turn of thought, and language of the perſon whoſe manner he
aſſumed*.

Of his abilities as a writer, I have had
ſo frequent occaſion to give my opinion

in

* I recollect a circumſtance, which will more fully
explain what I mean.

When I once came with him from the late Doctor
Johnſon's, I remarked that we had forgotten to mention
one of his old friends having juſt married a third wife.
I added, " What would the Doctor have ſaid to it!"
" Sir," replied Henderſon, " he would ~~would~~ have ſaid,
man is born to be deceived. We ſee daily inſtances
where expectation ſubdues experience. This will be
an additional example of the fallacy of hope, and diſap-
pointment of expectation. Yet we muſt allow the man
has *courage*, or after the ſufferings of two campaigns, he
would not voluntarily expoſe himſelf on the forlorn hope.
—*He will be blown up, Sir!*"

in this volume, that I will not repeat what has been already ſaid—I ſubmit them to the judgment of the reader.

He was a cloſe and acute reaſoner, and an expert logician. Though ignorant of the *names* of his weapons of argument, he could wield them with adroitneſs and power.

In the polite arts he had a good taſte; to an eye that quickly diſcerned defects in ſculpture, or painting, he joined a freedom of ridicule, which did not add to the number of his friends amongſt the ſecond claſs of artiſts.

His memory was uncommonly tenacious, and to that he was more indebted than to laborious ſtudy, or cloſe application, for in his early years he was indolent. But his

quickneſs

quickneſs of perception ſoon attained whatever he attempted, and once attained it became his own.

He uſed to expatiate on Dr. Johnſon's
tendency to ſuperſtition, and affected more
freedom of thinking than he poſſeſſed, for
he believed much which he would not acknowledge.

His ſpirits were generally high, but there
were hours, even after he had the moſt
flattering proſpects of fame and fortune,
when they ſunk into the loweſt depreſſion.*
Whether he acquired this tendency from
the

* At ſuch times he has often told me the following
ſtory :—When his brother was ten, and he not more
than eight years of age, their well being depending upon
the life of their mother, ſhe was afflicted with a violent
nervous

the books he read, or his difposition led him to fuch ftudies, I will not determine ; it is however certain that his reading was uncommonly

nervous diforder, which had funk her into a deep melancholy. While fuffering under this, fhe one morning left her houfe and children, who waited her return with impatience. Night approached, but their parent did not come. Full of terror, the two boys went in fearch of her. Ignorant what courfe to take, they wandered until midnight, about the places where fhe ufed to walk, but wandered without fuccefs. They agreed to return home, but neither of them knew the way. Fatigued, alarmed, diftreffed, they fat down on a bank to weep, when they obferved at fome diftance a luminous appearance, and fuppofing it a candle in fome friendly habitation, haftily directed their fteps towards it. As they moved, the light moved alfo, and glided from field to field, for a confiderable time. At length, it feemed fixed, and on their near approach, vanifhed on the fide of a large piece of water. On the margin, they found their mother in a ftate from which fhe was roufed by the prefence and tears of her children.

This

uncommonly multifarious. It compre-
hended all books upon apparitions, illusions
of the devil, and visions, from *Adye's Candle in the Dark* to *Calif's Wonders of the
invisible World.* He had trod the whole
circle of witchcraft, from *the History of the
Witch of Endor, to the Story of Mary
Squires.* Books of horror he had perused
from *Fox's Martyrology, to the Account
of the Dutch Cruelties at Amboyna.* To all
this he added a thorough knowledge of the
English classics, whose beauties he fully
conceived, and eminently displayed, by the
judgment, variety, and humour of his public readings. He knew the French language

---

This he has often asserted, he religiously believed to be
neither an *ignus fatuus*, nor a creation of the imagination,
but a kind interposition of Providence, for the pre-
servation of the widow, and the widow's sons.

·guage well, and fpoke it with great fluency and elegance.

His temper was placid, and under very uncommon government; I have not the recollection of ever having feen him in a paffion. He was not afhamed of obligations, but frequent in his acknowledgments.

In the acquirement of friends he was fortunate. The later years of his life were honoured with the notice of men from whofe converfation much was to be gathered, and his own equability of temper, and accomodating manners conciliated their regards.

If there was fometimes a little interchange of flattery, it was perhaps equally gratifying to each party. Henderfon faid, " it is the commerce of life, and when any one avows himfelf fo faftidious that

T   his

his mind revolts at such incense, we may fairly presume, he pretends to reject what was never offered, and rails at that branch of devotion, because he is not the object of it." He acknowledged it pleased him, and boldly asserted that no actor could perform well unless he was flattered, both in and out of the theatre. *

Like

* I think it was the late Mr. Topham Beauclerc, who inserted as a note in Cibber's Apology—That Mr. Garrick told him, when he read Lethe to his Majesty, he felt such a pressure upon his spirits, as disabled him from giving any force to the different characters of his own farce. His powers were frozen, and he was scarce capable of reading it to the conclusion. " Conceive to yourself, said he, a man wrapped up in a wet blanket reading a play to a king, and you will have a perfect idea of my situation."

This proves what Cibber asserts in his Apology, vol. 2. page 76. That *actors accustomed to loud and general plau-dits cannot exert themselves without.*

Like his predeceffor in his moft popular character, he was not averfe to the pleafures of a good table, and they were well beftowed upon him; he became exhilarated. I never faw him play Falftaff with fo much glee, as one evening of a lord-mayor's day, when he had dined and drank fack and fugar at the houfe of a friend. His eye was lighted up, and his whole countenance beamed voluptuous humour.

Having been early forced into the practice of ftrict œconomy, he was fully fenfible of the value of money, and acquired a habit of rejecting all expence which was not abfolutely neceffary, and the criterion was not his *income,* but his *wants.* With this attention the wages of his labour naturally accumulated, and confidering him as knowing fo well how to profit by his talents, he was

T 2

a fingular

fingular inftance of prudence being united with genius.

I think if he had lived as long as Mr. Garrick, he would have been at leaft as rich.

The letters and poems which follow; having no immediate connexion with the anecdotes, it was thought beft to infert them at the latter end of the volume. Thofe letters which are without dates, I have, near as my recollection enabled me, placed in the fame progreffion of time in which they were written.

To the Rev. Mr. P———.

London, October 1ſt, 1769.

I differ from you.—I believe objects of ſpeculation have more power to charm the ſoul from a ſenſe of its affliction, than *acts* of real and ſolid benevolence.

The greatneſs of mind which impels men to beneficent actions, prevents their dwelling upon them. When a man has acquired an habitual generoſity, and greatneſs of ſoul, the exerciſe of that generoſity, makes little or no durable impreſſion upon his mind; it is become a part of his nature, and performed without attention. It is not ſo with that ſpecies of wiſdom which impels the ſoul to dart into the regions of enquiry and inveſtigation. The ſpirits are agitated, the

T 3

paſſions

paſſions are engaged, and expand in the pur-
ſuit.—With what extacy does the mind glow
upon every new acquiſition.—How in a fine
frenzy rolling, doth it

> " Glance from heaven to earth,
> " From earth to heaven,
> " And as imagination bodies forth
> " The forms of things unknown,
> " Turns them to ſhape,
> " And gives to airy nothing,
> " A local habitation and a name."

Every faculty is in exertion—pain, ſick-
neſs, poverty, and all its conſequential
horrors, where are ye—ſunk, loſt, and trembling, at the throne of Genius.—What
but its wondrous potency could invigorate
ſo many great men, and turn the darkneſs
of their dungeon into light.

Hath

Hath not the soul continued its purſuits, with lank and fleſhleſs famine on one ſide, and reſtleſs juſtice, bearing in her hand an iron key, on the other. Gracious hea-ven! When affliction reareth the maſſy club! When oppreſſion ſhaketh the whip of ſcor-pions!—give me but one ſpark of this di-vine enthuſiaſm, and I will endure the blow. * * * * * * * * *
* * * * * * * * * * *,

To

To the Rev. Mr. P————.

London, December 21, 1769.

I HAVE received your prefent; I gave one of the pheafants to Mr. ———— I thank you for the other—I ate it where you were *cordially* drank to—make a pun of that, and you may fuppofe we toafted you in Geneva.

I have a defign in meditation, which if it fucceeds I fhall with promptitude convey to you. I reafon upon your temper from my own, and ftate you to myfelf as interefted in all my concerns.————Holland the comedian is dead, and ranting is no more.— Junius is outrageous, but vain is eloquence —obftinancy lofes all fenfes, but that of feeling.—

feeling.—I write this in poor fpirits and worfe health, an impertinent cold has fixed upon my throat, and a troublefome pain upon my head, and this I owe to Garrick's playing Haftings the other night.—I fhould be tempted to moralize here upon the conftant fucceffion of pain to entertainment, but that I will not ufurp your province.

I long to tranflate a fermon of Flechier's *upon Chriftmas-day;* I never met with an introduction fo fuitably majeftic, and language fo full of dignity—you may poffibly have it done by the next year, though I don't know whether it would fuit your audience.—There is another alfo, upon *the wife mens offerings,* which my heart burns to copy.—I never before confidered their offerings of gold, and myrrh, as emblematical, but only as prefents of honour and humility.

Mr.

Mr. D—— defires to be remembered to you; I gave him a hint of the thirty fermons you received. He looked a little difconcerted, and I believe repents his refufal. ——We have a new comedy; I have not feen it played, but I borrowed the pamphlet, and I do not recollect ever to have read any thing more dull and uninterefting, and yet it fucceeds with the town.

I am, &c.

J. HENDERSON.

To

To Mr. ————.

Who said, " He sometimes acted against the conviction
of his feelings, rather than be unlike the rest of the world."

.

London Dec. 25th.

" Dare to be wise,—begin,—for once begun,
" Your talk is easy,—half the work is done."

HORACE.

A S long as the modes of fashion continue to be repugnant to wisdom, this
counsel of Horace will deserve the closest
attention.   To steer against the popular current of error is indeed a noble daring.—A
mere speculative theorist, whose ideas are
gathered, more from the volume of recorded
incidents, than from the sphere they were
acted in, would think it unnecessary to

enjoin

enjoin men to dare to be, that which his books inform him every man struggles to be thought; but the man of the world sees instances every day, either in himself or others, where many opportunities of acquiring wisdom, or displaying it, are neglected, not from actual ignorance, or inaptitude of conception, but from an indolent or cowardly adherence to the reigning fashions of vice, error, impudence, or presumption.

True courage encreases with the prospect of danger. — That there is great danger in opposing the world in their most ardent pursuits, every one will allow who has ever felt the bitterness of neglect, or the poignancy of ridicule. The soul in almost every respect acts superior to the body; its sufferings are more acute, its pleasures more exquisite.—Many have by constitutional vigour dared to expose their persons to all the dan-

gers

gers of deſtructive war, whoſe ſpirits are ſo
ſubject to diſtreſs, that popular clamours, or
even the pen of an eſſayiſt, can hold them
in the continual perplexities of terror.

This argues a ſpecies of courage, very
different from bodily daring to be neceſſary
in Horace's advice, and a courage much
ſuperior too.

It has fallen within my obſervation, to
ſee impertinence and abſurdity, which
ſhocked the underſtanding of every one
except the ſpeaker, by mere dint of reſolute perſeverance change their forms, and
become, if not admired, at leaſt endured.
And indeed it hath been from ſuch a confident delivery, that impertinence and error
have forced their way into the world as
they have done. If folly can thus change
opinions, and render itſelf acceptable, how

much

much more so might wisdom.—I shall be told, perhaps, that their qualities are so different as to render the same modes of persuasion impracticable.—That error is presumptuous, and positive, and that the concomitants of wisdom, are meekness and diffidence.—I do not deny it.—Horace himself was of the same opinion, and therefore recommended it to them by the highest incitement of honour, to *dare* to be wise. He thought even meekness and diffidence virtues that were to be concealed, when the honour of wisdom was in question.—You may possibly quote our great model of christianity, as an instance of wisdom and meekness, united in the same person : but I beg leave to observe, that he never delivered his laws, or his injunctions with timidity—He suffered for his manly and bold advancement of them. He suffered with meekness, but gave laws with dignity, firmness, and vigour.—

The

—The world, I mean the enlightened part of it, have long since received his maxims, and blushed for the dishonour thrown upon the lawgiver.

Horace wrote in times very nearly resembling our own. Folly was popular in Rome, and so was courage; he therefore thought nothing so likely to stimulate his countrymen to wisdom, as an exertion of their favourite passion. He would have folly vanquished, and lie in chains, to encrease the triumphs of those who added kingdoms to the empire.

Philosophers have been ever accused of want of courage; I think Dryden somewhere calls them, cowards by profession. But in this instance, every one may become a hero. It belongs merely to the soul, and wisdom should be ashamed to nurse any opinion,

nion, which it dare not promulgate and de-
fend.

To ſhew of how great force example is
among us, I muſt remark that when a genius
riſes, he gives law to thouſands; kindles
imaginations that would have otherwiſe
ſunk into torpor, and warms thoſe pens,
which elſe would have frozen. It would
be the ſame, my friend, with every other
ſpecies of wiſdom—Do but dare to begin,
with a reſolute purpoſe and countenance; if
it does not anſwer, ſay there is no truth in

SHANDY.

To

To Mr. I———.

From the Banks of the Thames, June 18.

FOR the books you have my beſt thanks. I uſed to think I was fond of fiſhing, but I find it a very dull buſineſs. If the good gentleman of Uz had been devoted to my preſent ſituation, and fixed among ſuch a ſet of aquatic animals, his patience muſt have been exhauſted.* Sir, ſuch a life as I

U

now

---

* Doctor Franklin's opinion of angling, may be gueſſed at from the following ſtory, which the ſage often relates to thoſe he thinks *bit* with a taſte for *piſcatory delights.* About ſix o'clock one ſummer morning, (ſaid the philoſopher) as I was riding by the ſide of a running brook in America, I obſerved a gentleman with his fiſhing rod in his hand, a baſket, a bottle, and all the requiſites, by his ſide. I aſked him what ſport ?—I have

not

now lead, is fit for nothing but an otter, and I believe in my confcience the animals I am with are web footed, and have fins. They are neither fifh nor flefh, " *A man knows not where to have them,*" but yet I cannot quit thefe *rods,* and *earth worms,* thefe ten days. Think what a treafure was your parcel.

With Mifs Aikin's poems I am delighted, they abound in elegance and fublimity, and in harmony are not inferior to

Pope's

not been here more than two hours, was the anfwer.——When I returned at the clofe of the day, the fame gentle fwain was in exactly the fame place, and at the fame employment. I ftopped my horfe, and afked him if he had been well amufed ? " *Exceeding well,*" was the reply. —Have you caught many fifh ?—" Not any fir."—Had many bites ?——" No, not one bite, but I have had a moft glorious *nibble ! ! !*

Pope's. Indeed, if oppofed to the Effay on Man, *that* verfification is much excelled.

Until the arrival of your's, all the print I could pick up in the houfe, from garret to wine-cellar, was *Bracken's Farriery, Hannah Glaffes Cookery* (which by the way I very much like, for the *laft* receipt in the book is for a *furfeit) Pomfret's Poems,* and *Pope's Effay on Man;* which laft I have read through, and think it very inferior to his other ethic epiftles. It is wonderful that a man of fo exquifite a tafte, fo accurate an eye, and fo delicate an ear, fhould have deformed his pages, with fuch abbreviations as *Chanc'lor, Gen'ral, Conqu'rors, Pow'rs, Flow' s, Ev'ry, Heav'n;* I cannot fee how his lines are fhortened by them. *Heaven* will remain two fyllables in any mode I can pronounce it, let it be fpelled how you will. *Th' eternal, Th' apparent, T' inclofe,* and

innumerable

innumerable other examples might be quoted. The *philosophy* of the Essay I will not presume to meddle with, but the *poetry* is some of it very unworthy of Mr. Pope. Let us look at the first page.

> " The latent tracts, the giddy heights explore
> Of all who blindly creep, or *sightless* soar,
> Eye nature's walks, shoot folly as it flies,
> And catch the *manners living* as they rise."

Where a word ends with an *S*, a reader finds it unpleasant and difficult to begin the word following with the same serpentine letter. Would not *blindly soar*, have been equally poetical, and a better antithesis, than *sightless soar*. I should think *living manners* would have been quite as clear as *manners living*.—But this would be deemed high treason in the court of Parnassus, so " farewel it," till we meet.

The

The tranflations I have returned by the coach. I made feveral attempts to read them, but all in vain. I could not for the foul of me get thro' three pages. That you may not reproach me with returning the books without an opinion, take the following four lines. I .fcribbled them in the marginal leaf of the firft volume, but re- collecting myfelf, thought it would be more modefter to tear out the leaf, than let them remain in the front of the book, in my hand writing.

In holy church we fee divines tranflated,
And mitres oft' times grace the *empty pated*.
How hard, how very hard's an author's fate,
When *empty pated* fellows will tranflate.

If you could get hold of Pontoppidan's Norway, or Pierre Vaude, or Philip Quaries, (I don't mean the Emblem merchant) I

would

would thank you ; though we are likely to do somewhat better now, for a good pleasant fellow joined our *partie* this morning. I walked with him into the church-yard, but there was nothing worth the trouble of an Epitaph hunter.—He has given me one though which pleases me.   There is a good climax in it.   Have you ever seen it ?

Dr. Greenwood, his Epitaph on his Wife.

Ah Death ! Ah Death ! thou haft cut down,
The faireft *Green wood* in all this town ;
Her virtues and her good qualities are fuch,
She was worthy to marry a lord or a judge,
Yet fuch was her condefcenfion, and fuch her hu-
    mility,
She chofe to marry me, a Doctor in divinity,
For this heroic deed fhe ftands confeft,
Above all others the phœnix of her fex ;
And like that bird one young fhe did beget,
That fhe might not leave her fex difconfolate:
My grief for her lofs is fo very fore,
I can only write two lines more,

For

For this, and every other good woman's fake,
Never let a blifter be put on a lying-in woman's
back.

This is a ftrange patched letter, part
profe, part verfe, and part neither. But
whatever my letters are, believe that *I* am
with the moft profaic fincerity.

Your's,

J. HENDERSON.

 To

To Mr. I———.

Bath, Nov. 2, 1774.

AND fo you have been in France. Prithee Jack tell me, is there that difference in the faces, habits, and characters, of thefe people, which *appeareth in the lively pour-traitures we fee exhibited of them;* are their women either fo beautiful, or fo engaging as ours. I have not any great ambition to be-come either dominican, or capuchine, except that I might in either of thofe characters fee a nun *en defhabille.*

I fancy my face would be deemed too *friar-like* already, to be admitted as a *lay-brother,* but that thin, fafting, formal face of thine, would be pofitively a letter of re-commendation, and I think, my friend, you

would

would give an attentive ear to the confeſſions of the young *devote's*, and, upon proper terms, grant them abſolution. I wiſh I had been with you. I long to look at a noviciate;—but for a lady abbeſs—your deſcription hath ſatisfied me.

What you ſay of the French officers agrees with all I have ever heard. They are gentlemen by birth and education. The ſuperior carriage of the ſoldiers is owing to their being ſo univerſally taught fencing, an accompliſhment ſo uſeful, ſo neceſſary, but in this country ſo much neglected. As tactics have never been my ſtudy, I do not feel any great deſire to view their fortifications, notwithſtanding the great things you ſay of them. Marlborough was certainly a fine fellow, and reward was proportioned to his merit; but had even *he* planted twice the number of cannon he had

in

in France, againſt his own Blenheim, and employed *Monſieur Vauban* for his engineer, it would have ſtood the ſhock: ſo maſſy and ponderous is that huge heap of littleneſs, that I believe it will outlaſt the pyramids.

Can their churches exceed Weſtminſter Abbey?—Thoſe

  " Storied windows, richly dight,
  " Caſting a dim, religious light."

impreſs me with a kind of awe I do not feel in any other place. If I were an abſolute monarch, I would oblige ſuch of my ſubjects as had a fancy for erecting churches, to build them of the Gothic order.

'Tis ſtrange there ſhould be only one good picture at St. Omer's; but 'tis made up by plenty of *reliques*. I wiſh his Moſt Chriſtian Majeſty were viſited by a dream of heaven and

and Mortimer—But when Salvator's Witch
of Endor gives place to a Chinefe painting,
and that in the palace he inhabits !—what
can we expect ?

You fay *Louis Quatorze* will never be forgotten, though he had left no other me-
morial than the roads, planted and termi-
nated as they are ; yet, to an Englifhman,
after ten of their *poftes royales*, the profpect
moft devoutly to be wifhed is a good fupper,
which, it feems, you lacked.   But though
both H——s and you naufeated frogs, I
dare fay you relifhed Burgundy.   Yet the
juice of the grape, without fome folids,
would fhrink a Falftaff to a Mafter Slender.
After all, a capon and a cup of fack, are
better than fnails and Champagne.   Such
meagre fare and cold potations——" I
hate it."

I am

I am now going to dine with a Jew : *his*
will be a *Mosaic* treat. Fish, with oil instead
of sauce, and a turkey stuffed with garlick
was our last feast. *This* may, perhaps, be
a boiled goose and pease-pudding, a stew of
venison in sour cyder, and a mutton-sausage
pasty. I wish the worthies of old would
have considered, before they made so many
laws about eating, that though the tables of
the law were very properly in their depart-
ments, the dining tables *seemed* more peculiarly
in the province of the ladies. If prohibiting
what is good be a sin, which I firmly believe
it is, both Moses and Pythagoras have much
to answer for. They banished beans and
bacon between them, and that, let me tell
you, is no bad dish when a man is hungry,
in spite of *their philosophy*.

I suppose the women are returned, heavy
laden with the labours of the loom and the

spoils

ſpoils of the nunnery, and, I hope, eſcaped the Cuſtom-houſe inſpectors. Farewel: if you, or your *cara ſpoſa*, will return me as much, and as complete nonſenſe as I have written, I will acknowledge that you have not travelled in vain, nor ſurveyed ſtrange countries for nought.

Your's, ever,

J. H.

To Mr. I————.

Bath, October 10th.

I BEG your excuse for my silence, but I have such a multitude of business upon my mind, that it takes away my power, and abates much of my inclination to write.

You must not be offended at this, because it contains no disrespect or abatement of the sincere and just affection I have for you.—Make my compliments and thanks to Mrs. ———— for the waistcoat, which is ten times more admired than I am, and the girls will run the length of the parade, to see my flower'd and gilt belly, who would not quit their own threshold to see me. Foote is down here, and I have talked to

him

him a good deal, and dined at a gentleman's where he was, Garrick wrote a letter to Mr. Taylor the other day, which I
faw, 'and he fpeaks very handfomely of me.
———I play away here in the old way; I
played one new character laft week, (Pierre)
and am preparing with all my might and
main for twelve more at leaft. Doctor
Dodd is here, and I have dined with him
too. Defire Mrs. ——— to believe I love
her, and to leave off abufing me as fhe ufed
to do, and do you think me unalterably,

Your's,

J. HENDERSON.

To

To Mr. I———.

Bath, 2d May.

T H A N K S, thanks, thanks for your
care about my mother—you make me very
eafy by telling me you intereft yourfelf for
her———I cannot write long letters nor good
ones now, fo you muft be content with
friendly ones.

It is now one of the firft wifhes of my
heart that *———* may fwing, for who-
ever injures my dear friend *———* fhall
have all the bitternefs of my foul attend
him.—Why or wherefore is no matter.———
If I had intereft with the devil, (which by
the bye I believe I never fhall have) I would
beg a double portion of remorfe and internal
torment for that rafcal.

To

To Mr. I———,

Birmingham, July 8, 1776.

My Dear I——,

IT is very strange to me, that my mother should not have received my letters. I wrote to her the day before I set out for this place. I told her of my design to pass my summer here—However, on the receipt of your's, I have again written to her. If that letter also should miscarry, pray, my dear friend, tell her that it invited her to live with me at Bath. It told her, that I would procure her an apartment in the same house with me if I could; if not, I will provide her with a lodging near me: but I rather think and hope, that we may live together. I shall be there the latter end of September. There is nothing in my power which I

X

would

would not do, to make that excellent woman happy—She and you Jack, have but one fault, and that is, too great a partiality for a very filly fellow—But be that as it may, I shall be uneasy 'till I have her with me. As to yourself, my worthy friend, I scarce know what to say; my heart longs to talk with you, but its fensations are so simple, and so boyish, I know not how to write them. I love your peace, your happiness, and would I could promote it: I love *————* too; pray tell her so: tell her that no one on earth, except thyself, my friend, can have a better sense of her deserving, or a truer affection for her.

Adieu,

J. HENDERSON.

To Mr. I———.

Birmingham, July 26, 1776.

DEAR I———,

I HAVE received a letter from my mother, which I have really had no time to anſwer, and now I know not where ſhe is. Perhaps you do, for ſhe tells me ſhe ſhould go to London. She objects to coming to Bath, on account of the weight of her baggage, and the expence of its carriage; but that is nothing. Pray tell her, Jack, that I ſhall be two ſeaſons more at Bath, by articles, and I had rather have her with me, than that ſhe ſhould be liable to inconveniences elſewhere. I find that ſhe has been very ill treated in the country, and my heart aches to think of it; for if there ever was unaffected and genuine ſimplicity,

                and

and innocence of heart, it is in my mother.
I shall not be at ease if I have her not with
me; for I not only feel a sense of duty, but
a lively and tender affection for her—I know
her peculiarities, and can indulge them better than any other person, and I think it will
give her happiness to see and know my
manner of living, &c. Do, my dearest
friend, tell her what I say, and if she wants
money let her have it, and I will send you
a draft for it without delay.

Believe me,

Your's, &c.

J. H.

To

To Mr. I———.

Birmingham, Aug. 31, 1776.

Dear I——,

I HAVE had letters from my mother, who will be with me at Bath—She will go through London, and if she calls on you, which I defired her to do, I know your friendfhip will fupply her with any money fhe may want, and I will remit it to you.

Mrs. Yates is here at prefent, and we played *The Wonder* laft night. You cannot imagine how I am carreffed by all ranks of people. I fhall leave this place covered with Birmingham laurels.

I play with Mrs. Yates again on Monday, *The Roman Father*, and moft probably

X 3   Shylock

Shylock afterwards. Things are ripening for me; I am not sorry, even now, that I did not come to London. The end will shew I shall do very well—I am, in the mean time, as happy as I have any notion of being. I wish we could have a day or two together; but for that we must wait.

Farewell,

J. HENDERSON.

To Mr. I———.

* * * * * * * * * * * * * * * *

* * *. I am very ill at this writing, and have been ſo this week ; but it will go away, or Doctor Schomberg and I, with a reinforcement of apothecaries, will drive it away—I hope you and *———* are in health ; there is no one's health dearer to me,

Did I tell you that I have got my mother here, and am combating with her legion of gloomy blue D———s too ; but I ought to do it, and that is enough for me.

Adieu,

X 4   J. H.

To the Reverend Mr. D——

Bath, Feb, 17th, 1776,

Dear Doctor,

I SCARCE know how to begin a letter, I long to write to you; I have many times been about to addreſs you, and though I never wanted, nor ever ſhall want a ſub-ject, if I were to write all that my heart feels towards you; yet after a certain time has elapſed in ſilence, one knows not how to reſume the ſame familiarity, and with the ſame ſpirit, as if no chaſm had been made in our correſpondence; at leaſt I feel it ſo.— I ſhould hardly have had courage now if Mr, ——— had not told me you thought it unkind in me to be ſilent—I would do almoſt any thing to remove ſuch an opinion

from

from your mind, for I love and honour you with sincere attachment, and respect. "Something too much of this,"

I shall not wonder if you join with all my friends in town, to condemn my staying here in preference to being in London, because I hear the business has been very partially explained, but I think if it were fairly and fully disclosed to you, I should rather have your approbation. I am naturally timorous, and have an instinctive reluctance to engage in bustle, contention, and intrigue. I have no talents for them, and therefore think it would not be prudent to quit the moderate and quiet path I am in, for such hazardous pursuits. I will tell you, my most dear friend, the simple principle on which I acted, and I think it almost an *axiom*. If I am really wanted on the London stage, I ought to be placed there on honourable and advantageous terms, and I should be fo. If I am *not* really wanted, I have no bufinefs there, nor can the defign of having me there be other than treacherous and pernicious. Yet farther. It was only propofed to engage me for one year; a propofal by which the manager hazarded nothing, as the very novelty of one who had been talked of as I had been, would have paid in very few nights the falary I was to receive; and *I hazarded every thing by it.*

My friend W————* tells me he has thoughts of taking orders, a view which I am perfuaded you will encourage, and promote, as he certainly has not, any more than myfelf, talents for bufinefs and chicane; I was very fenfibly touched with his misfortunes, and think the church is the only afylum he can meet with from

them

them.   But you will judge better than I can.

I hope, my dear friend, you have health, and that is all I need wish to such a heart, and such a capacity as yours ; felicity and honour will naturally follow such goodness, and such understanding, if their operations are not retarded by sickness.

Believe me, &c.

J. HENDERSON.

*Inscribed under the Picture of a Lady who
had slighted the Author.*

(Written in 1769.)

ONWARD it presses with an eager view,
More splendid scenes, and transports to pursue;
Far as ambition's piercing eye can see,
Nor once regards humility and me.
No gentle blandishments arrest its speed,
Nor once it stops, though love and meekness bleed,
Bleed in its path, and tremble in its course,
Weak ties have love, against ambition's force.

By pleasure urg'd—urg'd by ambition's sting,
From love, from me, from tenderness you spring,
Your picture, faithful to your heart as face,
Eludes my grasp, and mocks my fond embrace.
No more from solemn thought to mirth I fly,
No more the heart exults, no more the eye
Darting abroad, collects each scattered ray,
Which humour beam'd, and fancy led astray.

Inscribed

Inscribed under a Print of Orpheus playing
on his Lyre, being the Frontispiece to a
young Lady's Music Book.

(Written in 1768.)

W H E N Orpheus sung, or sweetly touch'd his lyre,
Such heav'n born sounds the woods and groves inspire ;
The rugged rocks, and wood-clad mountains dance,
And wild with pleasure, at his song advance ;
Such melody stern Pluto's soul disarms,
From Pluto's throne Eurydice it charms.
At length by cruel hands bereav'd of breath,
(For music's self cannot contend with death)
The shepherds all their rural sports forsook,
And every eye assum'd a mournful look,
Each nymph felt anguish—grief felt ev'ry swain,
In place of harmony, see discord reign.
Long in this state men liv'd, and had remain'd
So new——But you, my fair, have deign'd
To sooth our cares, and soften all our grief,
And brought sweet melody to our relief.

So

So ſoft the ſounds, of grace and eaſe poſſeſt,
Such airs mellifluous humanize each breaſt,
No longer need you envy Orpheus' fame,
Since a new Orpheus reigns in *———'s name.

A Receipt to make a Paſtoral.

TAKE firſt two handfuls of wild thyme,
Or any herb that ſuits your rhyme,
And ſhred it finely o'er your plains,
Fit to receive your rolling ſwains.
With crocus, violets, and daiſies,
Be ſure to fill the vacant places;
Then plant your groves and myrtle bowers,
(Well water'd with celeſtial ſhowers)
And, to avoid the critics quarrel,
A ſprig or two of Virgil's laurel.
Your ground thus laid, your trees thus plac'd,
Sweeten'd with flow'rs to your taſte,
Your ſhepherd take, and as is wont,
Baptize him at the poet's font.
Adorn him with ſcrip, crook, and reed,
And lay him by for farther need.

Then take a damsel neat and fair,
And in a fillet bind her hair;
Give her a flock of tender sheep;
And keep her by you—She will keep.

An Imitation of a French Pastoral.

I

DAPHNIS one day his flock had led
  Into a verdant grove :
Not far off; Phillis in the shade,
  Had brought her lambs to rove :
Both of them met each other,
    Her Daphnis saw,
    Him Phillis saw,
Each of them saw the other.

II.

Good day, sweet sheepherdess, said he,
  Shepherd said she good day,
In yonder orchard prithee see,
  The grass how fresh and gay :

Both

Both inftantly went thither ;
    Daphnis fat down,
    Phillis fat down,
They both fat down together.

III.

A nofegay then of violets made,
    For Phillis the fhepherd pull'd,
Phillis for him, in order laid
    Some flowers nicely cull'd,
Both offer'd them each other ;
    Her's, Daphnis took,
    His, Phillis took,
Each took them of the other.

IV.

Permit, upon thy breaft, he cry'd,
    That I this nofegay place,
With mine the pretty lafs replied,
    I'd fain thy bofom grace.
Both granted one another ;
    His, Daphnis plac'd,
    Her's, Phillis plac'd, .
Each plac'd them on the other.

V.

To ever true and conſtant be,
   Make me, ſaid he, a vow,
To conſtant be, and true, ſaid ſhe,
   The ſame to me do thou;
Both promis'd one another,
    This Daphnis did,
    This Phillis did,
They did ſo by each other.

The

The following little Fragment he wrote soon
after his arrival at Bath. There is, I
think, a sort of whimsical humour about
it, somewhat resembling the *Historie*
which Mr. Henderson read into reputation : but as neither John Gilpin's Race,
nor Mr. Henderson's very *outré* manner
of reading it, ever gave me any very
extatic pleasure, I think some apology
necessary to the reader, for inserting an
imperfect Ballad.

A New Ballad.

YE lords and lordlings lend an ear,
   No wicked lies I write,
The truth most truly you shall hear,
   For your ease and delight.

In Bath a wine-merchant did dwell,
   And C——y was his name,
Who by the blessing of the muse,
   I now transmit to fame.

This wine-merchant a daughter had,
  A daughter brown had he,
Who when she wore both cap and shoes,
  Reach'd to her father's knee.

When other misses dreft their dolls,
  She dreft her mind, I ween,
And when her play-mates made dirt pies,
  She at her book was seen.

Full broad the ribband which she wore,
  To bind her head around,
And right fantastic were the shoes,
  Which kept her from the ground.

And now, when time had form'd her ear,
  To music she it bent,
And pleas'd the neighboring gentles all,
  And all folks where she went.

Her father grew exceeding proud,
  Exceeding proud grew he,
And ask'd the gentles all around,
  His daughter for to see.

Y 2

Hoping

Hoping, that some of noble birth,
 Would be caught by a song,
And careless of her low estate,
 In wedlock bind her strong.

The gentles star'd, and knew not what
 To do, or what to say;
They wip'd their faces as they could,
 They bow'd, and came away.

Now see how pride destroyeth all
 The knowledge God hath sent,
Sith he who serv'd full many a man,
 Could harbour such intent.

For once, before his heart grew proud,
 A livery he wore,
And us'd to wait with hat in hand,
 His master to the door.

So well he did in this behave,
 So humble then did seem,
That no one thought of pride or state,
 This merchant e'er could dream.

The

The nobles, therefore, notic'd him,
   And bought his wine, to shew
That merit they would patronize,
   Though sprung from ne'er so low.

Yet all this while no lordling came,
   With offer of his hand,
Nor squireling spruce, nor parson trim,
   With cassock and with band.

What shall I do, the father cry'd,
   My daughter will grow old,
And all her wit, and all her voice,
   Will serve her but to scold.

Then to the synagogue went he,
   And brought out many a Jew,
To hear her play, and hear her sing,
   And of her take a view.

From Pontus, and from Phrygia,
   From Cappadocia eke,
These wandering pilgrims came I ween,
   Two or three times a week.

They

They fat, they heard, and took their fnuff,
  And wondering, roll'd their eyes,
And then protefted,—that without
  Some wine they could not rife.

Then Franco thin, and Cappa fat,
  Declar'd upon their word,
They thought her for a Jew too good,
  And bid her wed a lord.

But now comes on a dreadful tale,
  I tremble to relate,
Oh, that fome lord, or bifhop had,
  Torn out this leaf of fate.

To Bath there came a ftrange young man,
  Nobody knew from whence;
Prefuming on fome foolifh gifts,
  Of talent and of fenfe.

Unto the playhoufe ftraight he went,
  The manager to fee,
Who gave immediately confent,
  A player he fhould be.

The

The day was fixt, the day was come,
  That he fhould firft appear,
When lo in Hamlet as he ftood,
  He fhook his hat with fear.

This damfel faw, this damfel figh'd,
  And bath'd her jetty eyes,
And faid, my heart is near breaking,
  For Hamlet when he dies.

The father ftorm'd, and lock'd his doors,
  This player to prevent,
Swore, like Ophelia, fhe fhould drown,
  Before he'd give confent.

But fay what bolts or bars, can keep
  A woman from her will ;
'Tis more than mortal man can do,
  * * * * * * * * * *.

Cætera defunt.

            EPIGRAM

EPIGRAM

On Artaxerxes, and other Operas, performed at the Theatres.

OUR English stage, which was at first design'd,
To raise the genius, and improve the mind,
To expose the various follies of the town;
Seems *now* contented to expose *its own*.

The Blighted Wreath.

VIVID and green, the laurel Roscius wore,
Still water'd with the foftering dew of praise,
  'Till vanity and avarice fwore,
To have a pluck at his long-envied bays.

They waited on him—welcome guefts they were,
And artful, took poffeffion of his heart;
  Then ftrove to blaft, the wreath they could not tear,
With venom foul, infus'd by fpecious art.

Moft

Moſt natural magic, and dire property,
Alas, too plainly to the world were ſeen,
    On wholeſome fame uſurp'd immediately,
And ſickly yellow gain'd upon the green.

    Almoſt, each night, ſome leaf its verdure loſt,
Yet they his weak and cred'lous heart conſol'd ;
    They bade him prize his laurel by its coſt,
When ev'ry leaf ſhould be transform'd to gold.

    Pernicious alchemy ! ah, treacherous friends,
How could you, nature's darling thus deceive ;
    That you have compaſs'd your inſidious ends,
The ſoul of Shakeſpeare, and the muſe ſhall grieve.

    Ah, what avails it, that on Thames's ſhore,
Three hundred thouſand pounds his banker keeps,
    Whilſt Phœbus and the Muſes all deplore,
His avarice waking, whilſt his genius ſleeps.

    Theſe pounds, indeed, will many a flatterer buy ;
But ah ! where then are brother George's hopes ;
    Theſe pounds, were doom'd his children to ſupply,
Not pay for ſcribbling *metaphors* and *tropes.*

An

An *Impromptu* on Mr. GARRICK's
Funeral.

AS from the borders of Cocytus' wave,
Not yet enfranchis'd by the clofing grave, *
Garrick juft peep'd into the world above,
And faw a fombrous long proceffion move ;
Saw the ftrand glitter with the tawdry ftate,
Part grave, part gay, part tinfel, and part plate ;
The prim deportment of lugubrious mutes,
And the taught toffings of the feather'd brutes.

    " Another jubilee, he cried, appears,
" Go bid the managers difmifs their fears ;
" No more from empty theatres defpair,
" And dread of duns, deliver to the air !
" Call all my carpenters—bid George attend,
" And ranfack Monmouth-ftreet from end to end ;
" Buy all the blacks, defraud the ftarving moth,
" Or let him, if he will, defile the cloth :
" Bring moth and all—we have no time to lofe—
" If there's not black enough, then buy the blues.

" Dye

" Dye all the truncheons, and their edges gild,

" All but that truncheon I was wont to wield ;

" Buy from the paftry-cooks their twelfth-night flags,

" To flame in front, the rear be cloth'd with rags ;

" The dirtieft wardrobe will the rear fupply,

" Our ftage perfpective will deceive the eye :

" All to your feveral offices repair,

" Whilft I determine—in what place or where,

" This gaudy mummery may beft appear.

" If for Ophelia, by young Hamlet mourn'd ;

" Or for poor Juliet, yet alive inurn'd."

Thus far he fpoke, in an imperial tone,
And quite forgot the funeral was his own.

Alas, poor Garrick, in Elyfian meads,
Where new delight to new delight fucceeds ;
Still fhall the phantom wealth thy fteps purfue,
And tinge thy pleafures with a *careful* hue.

The two foregoing Jeu d'Efprits I feveral
years ago fubmitted to the infpection of my
friend, Mr. Mickle, whofe tranflation of
the

the Lusiad will remain a monument of his poetic talents, while this country retains taste for luxuriant imagery, adorned with harmonius numbers—He thought that they contained much wit, but more severity, and hoped that Mr. Garrick's various powers as an actor, and generosity as a friend, would be held in remembrance, when his little foibles, as a man, were forgotten; and that it was rather unfair to lash *his* memory for the gaudy mummery of a funeral, originating in the folly and ridiculous vanity of surviving friends. " I will show you (said he) what is my opinion of Mr. Garrick," and gave me the following lines.

Upon Mr. GARRICK.

By Mr. MICKLE.

FAIR was the graceful form Prometheus made,
Its front, the image of the God difplayed:
All heaven approved it, e'er Minerva ftole
The fire of Jove, and kindled up the foul.

So Shakefpeare's page, the flower of poefy,
E'er Garrick rofe, had charms for every eye;
'Twas nature's genuine image, wild and grand,
The ftrong marked picture of a mafter's hand.

But when *bis* Garrick—Shakefpeare's Pallas came,
The Bard's bold painting burft into a flame:
Each part, new force and vital warmth received,
As touched by heaven—and all the picture lived.

ERRATA.

Page.	Line.		
15	2	*read* circumstances—*for* circumstance.
22	3	thy	thine.
42	8	he	it.
45	7, and 8—should not be divided, but the same paragraph continued.		
91	12	*read* hands————*for* stands.
105	18	witches	wishes.
125	3	wit	wits.
138	2	Dec. 22, 1774	Oct. 24, 1772.
196	7	manner in which he—manner he.
196	8	justified	satisfied.
218	2	1778	1780.
224	4	unwillingly	unwilling.
290	11	are not inferior	not inferior.
294	12	were	are.